A COAT OF MANY COLORS

Putting Jewish Characters on Stage

ROY SCHREIBER

A COAT OF MANY COLORS

PUTTING JEWISH CHARACTERS ON STAGE

ISBN: 979-8-35093-201-0

Contents

INTRODUCTION 1

SHYLOCK REVISITED 5

GOOD DEEDS..23

MARGERY MEETS HARRY.......................75

EDUCATING HENRY ADAMS 127

THE OPTIMIST.................................. 187

Introduction

It hangs on. Like a piece of old chewing gum stuck under a desk. For reasons old and new, even after a couple of thousand years. Antisemitic stereotypes refuse to vanish. Why?

Is it a chicken and egg problem? Are Jewish people victims of negative stereotyping or does the hatred of them spark their negative stereotype?

It comes down to this: To the anti-Semite, in the worst possible ways, all Jews are alike and not really human.

Probably the most famous Jewish theatrical character, Shylock, tries to undermine this negative image: "If you prick us, do we not bleed?" With this line, Shakespeare says what so many in his world and beyond doubted. Jews are part of humanity.

The Jewish characters in the plays found here emphasize that humanity in another way. Their differences from one another are more significant than their similarities:

In *Shylock Revisited* the title character won't give up his efforts to make the merchant of Venice, Antonio, pay what he owes. In *Good Deeds* a screen writer, Salka Viertel, pays the price for helping Nazi era Jewish artists escape from Europe. Harry Houdini takes on and outwits a reluctant con woman in *Margery Meets Harry*. *Educating Henry Adams* has the queen of Tahiti convince the U.S. historian, Henry Adams, to help her write a family history, even though it leaves out her Jewish heritage. And finally, in *The Optimist*, a Jewish college professor discovers that the world goes beyond the logical solutions he thinks will solve all problems.

Just like the Biblical Joseph, with his multi-colored coat, many of these Jews pay a price for their position in the wider world.

Another key question needs asking: Who is Jewish? The attempts to find an answer vary at least as much as the nature of these Jewish stage characters.

Looked at from the non-Jewish perspective, the answer to the question has one of two answers: heritage or religious belief.

Some tried to have it both ways. Going back a couple of centuries, the Jewish born British Prime Minister, Benjamin Disraeli, worshiped in the Anglican church. He looked at himself as a Christian. No longer of the Jewish faith.

Yet he could flaunt his Jewish heritage. Disraeli reputedly told a group of British aristocrats that, while their most distant ancestors painted themselves blue and ran half naked through the forest, his wrote the Bible.

Toward the end of his life, Disraeli attended a diplomatic conference of world powers. There he encountered Otto von Bismark the German chancellor. After the conference ended, Bismarck said, "The old Jew. He's the one." For him, clearly, Jewish heritage mattered most.

That view has predominated. The Nazis took it to the ultimate extreme, to their Final Solution, to the Holocaust.

Yet, despite the Nazis, an important segment of the world, but only a segment, still put worship before heritage. Many Roman Catholic priests, including Pope Pius XII, tried to save Jewish converts to their religion from the Nazi death camps. They had little or no success. For non-Jews, nearly a century on, their view remains in the minority.

Looked at from inside the Jewish world, what outsiders see as a simple dichotomy becomes much more complicated. As the saying goes, "Where there are two Jews, there are three opinions." That is why it is possible to find Jews defining who is Jewish in a wide variety of ways.

For starters, anyone with a Jewish parent is Jewish. Then again, only those with a Jewish mother are Jewish. Some say anyone who converts from another religion becomes Jewish. Others believe that only those born to members of orthodox congregations and who worship in their synagogues are Jewish. For still others, without joining a congregation of any description, they accept Jewish culture and consider themselves Jewish.

Something gets lost in these internal disputes. Even using the widest, most encompassing definition, the Jewish people represent a tiny portion of the world's population. Except for the first, none of the multiple Jewish views on their identity have migrated very far beyond Jewish ranks.

Yet, despite the small numbers, at one time or another Jewish people have attracted negative attention from all over the world. Not too many years ago, the radical nationalist Japanese group, Aum Shinrikyo, put forth antisemitic views.

Various Jewish groups turn inward in an effort shut out the wider world and its views of them. It doesn't work. The wider world has its ways of overwhelming even the most determined efforts to reject it. Pretending antisemitism doesn't matter or even exist, won't make it go away.

Even for activist groups, internal problems can bring efforts to a halt. When conflicting attitudes toward Israel and/or its government reach the forefront, progress does not describe what goes on. Any number of U.S. community and college groups spend more time fighting each other than antisemitism.

That shouldn't mean everyone gives up. Given its long history, antisemitism is unlikely to fade away on its own. It makes sense to try to get rid of it in a variety of ways.

In doing so, pointing out and condemning antisemitic statements and actions has its place. Many commentators do condemn these outrages. They point to the lives and careers that suffer. They point to injured and dead people. Yet, whatever good the commentary does, their commentary comes after-the-fact.

And, frustratingly, among the anti-Semites, the public condemnation, even arrests and convictions, only burnish their credentials. They claim martyrdom and use it to draw others to their cause. Of late, social media gives them a new, often untraceable, outlet for antisemitic speech and incitement. And the incidents go on.

In order to undermine the spread of this attitude with so many years of belief behind it, non-Jews need to believe that Jewish people have much in common with them. That to condemn Jews as a group is to condemn themselves. To make that case, everyone needs to see Jewish people as individuals, as fellow human beings, not as a faceless group.

The historically based Jewish characters found in the following plays won't be confused with each other. Of equal importance, all the principal characters (several of the minor ones) are based on actual people. Why? Because if these Jewish characters aren't real, if they are imaginary, the case for the coat of many colors as a metaphor for the Jewish world falls apart.

Granted it is something of a stretch to view Shylock as an actual historical figure. Yet he seems to live in history as much as he does on stage. Shakespeare has a talent like few of any era. He makes his character memorable and seemingly real. No historian writing about Richard III can ignore Shakespeare's image of him.

The characters in these plays are meant to continue what Shakespeare started. Through Shylock he showed all of us that we have a shared humanity. Before Shakespeare, the very humanly portrayed Joseph received the gift of a coat of many colors and suffered the consequences. He provides the template for the Jewish people who came after him.

Famously, Shakespeare wrote that all the world is a stage and we are but actors upon it. These plays present that statement in reverse. The stage becomes the world and the actors are the human beings in it.

Note:

Most of the plays that follow went through either the Script Lab at Chicago Dramatists and/or the Plays in Progress program of the Dramatists Guild. All of these shows received public readings at either Chicago Dramatists or Naked Angels, Chicago. NPR, college/university and community stations broadcast *The Optimist*. SAG-AFTRA actors and professional musicians perform all the roles. The show is available as an audio book on Audacity and Amazon Audible Books.

SHYLOCK REVISITED

CHARACTERS:

Daughter
Father
Jessica
Shylock
Portia/Balthasar
Antonio

Scene 1

Scene: *Lights come up on SHYLOCK, wearing jeans and a t-shirt, a long beard and wig with payot (side curls). Nearby is JESSICA, a much younger actor. She also wears, jeans and a t-shirt and a heavy, beaded necklace with a large metal cross at the end. FATHER and DAUGHTER enter. He wears slacks and a sport shirt. She has on a modern day punk style outfit. Also visible are tattoos and bright florescent purple hair.*

FATHER: Okay. You dragged me down here to see them. I've seen them.

> [*Waves a hand in the direction of the actors.*
> *Then turns and starts to leave.*]

DAUGHTER: Come on dad. Be nice. You've done Shakespeare a million times. I want t' know what you think about the play. Really.

FATHER:

> [*Father stops.*]

You think you can improve on Shakespeare. Really?

DAUGHTER: Merchant of Venice feels like he stitched together a couple of one act plays.

FATHER: Well he didn't. His followed his sources. More or less.

DAUGHTER: Three mystery boxes and a mean practical joke about a ring dumped in with a Jew who wants revenge. Maybe he shouldn't 've followed his sources, more or less.

FATHER: So what are you trying do to? Exactly.

DAUGHTER: Just listen. You'll see. Okay?

> [*The father reluctantly nods, yes.*]

DAUGHTER:

[*To the actors.*]

Now.

[*Through the rest of the play, whenever actors speak to each other, stage lights stay on them and dim, but do not go out, on the other actors not involved in the action.*]

JESSICA: I'm surprised you let me in.

SHYLOCK: I am surprised you are here.

JESSICA: I know you'll find it hard to believe, but I care about what happens to you.

SHYLOCK: You stole from me. Abandon me to practice heresy. This is how you show you care.

JESSICA: The Bible tells Jews and Christians to honor their fathers.

SHYLOCK: You honor your Jewish father by robbing him and going off with a Christian.

JESSICA: What I did has nothing to do with how I feel about you.

SHYLOCK; In our community what you did weighs on me.

JESSICA: We could go with "sticks and stones", or I could just say let 'em talk.

FATHER: Whoa, whoa.

[*Lights go up on father and daughter.*]

FATHER: This is supposed to improve Shakespeare? What kind of language is this?

DAUGHTER: The days of iambic pentameter are long gone.

FATHER: It's what an audience expects from a play called The Merchant of Venice.

DAUGHTER: Everyone knows that title. Besides, I think Shakespeare's copyright expired.

FATHER: The first time an actor says your line, half your audience will head for the exits.

DAUGHTER: Okay. How about calling the play Shylock? Everyone knows him too.

FATHER: Shylock Revisited.

DAUGHTER: Good. That I can live with. Shall we?

[*Daughter signals players to start.*]

SHYLOCK: You are not the one who hears the talk about your so-called marriage.

JESSICA: I didn't get married to prove a point.

SHYLOCK: Even though you go off with that Christian.

JESSICA: Lorenzo

SHYLOCK: His name doesn't matter. For me, both of you have become ghosts.

JESSICA: I've heard you consider me dead.

SHYLOCK: If you heard I went to the synagogue and had the rabbi say prayers for the dead, you heard a lie.

JESSICA: I never thought you'd do that.

SHYLOCK: You contradict yourself.

JESSICA: Not really. After mother died, I can remember the rabbi coming up to you on the street and begging for your yearly donation. You turned your back on him and walked away.

SHYLOCK: Money has nothing to do with it.

JESSICA: You want me to believe that money doesn't matter to you.

SHYLOCK: The rabbi prayed over my dead sons. My Leah too. Enough.

JESSICA: Maybe if I was your son, things would've been different between us.

SHYLOCK: I gave you all the freedoms you could ever want. Just like a son.

JESSICA: And I never complained about how you treated me.

SHYLOCK: The world knows God's reward for my good deed. Why have you come back?

JESSICA: To make you a proposal.

SHYLOCK: A term that implies money.

JESSICA: Money, among other things.

SHYLOCK: I will listen.

JESSICA: I'll give back the turquoise ring mother you gave in return for a favor. One that 'll make you money.

SHYLOCK: Let me understand what you are saying. Leah's first gift to me. One of the many things you stole. Now you will return it. For a favor.

JESSICA: Yes.

SHYLOCK: What favor?

JESSICA: Take the money Bassanio offers you to pay off Antonio's loan. Forget putting Antonio on trial.

SHYLOCK: No.

JESSICA: You say without a moment of hesitation

SHYLOCK: If he did not pay the money back, in front of witnesses, he made an agreement with me to forfeit an alternative.

JESSICA: Taking a pound of flesh that will kill him.

SHYLOCK: He agreed. I will have it.

JESSICA: Flesh over money. I thought I knew you.

FATHER: This is too much.

[*Lights come up on father and daughter.*]

I can see where you're going.

DAUGHTER: By too much you mean unexpected. Right?

FATHER: This is the story of a persecuted man who wants to push his persecutors too far. If you have Jessica win this argument, there's no play.

DAUGHTER: And you realize at this minute, right here in the good old U.S., a play about a Jew who wants to kill a Christian feeds into all those stupid stereotypes about Jews that won't go away.

FATHER: If he takes Jessica's offer, you feed into the one that we're supposed to be a bunch of money grubbers.

DAUGHTER: Shakespeare's Shylock is another version of the Jew who eats little Christian children's blood in his matzo.

FATHER: Shakespeare didn't write the play to make points about religious politics. He writes about the characters as people.

DAUGHTER: He had no choice.

FATHER: Of course he had a choice.

DAUGHTER: Some choice. If he messed up politically, religiously, he got thrown in the Tower or whatever. These days, not my worry.

FATHER: Let's see what happens in the next election.

DAUGHTER: If I make Shylock a someone who pushes too far and then pulls back, that piece of humanity rubs off on the rest of us.

FATHER: That isn't Shakespeare's Shylock. [Pause] I've changed my mind. Take his name out of the title.

DAUGHTER: If I give the lead character a new name, it'll mean I need to do the same for all the others.

FATHER: Then do it.

DAUGHTER: If I do, it won't matter.

FATHER: It most certainly will.

DAUGHTER: Anyone who's a Shakespeare fan 'll figure out it's Shylock and company.

FATHER: I don't see a problem with that.

DAUGHTER: And I don't see what's wrong with asking, "What if?" about Shylock.

[*Daughter signals the actors to resume.*]

SHYLOCK: Already you sound like a Christian.

JESSICA: Bassanio and Antonio are my friends.

SHYLOCK: So, you offer me Leah's ring as a favor for them.

JESSICA: I've watched you bargain. You offer what matters most to your buyer. For a high price.

SHYLOCK: And you think playing the role of bargaining thief will make up for all you've taken from me?

JESSICA: Let's forget about the ring for now. A Jewish match for me. How much would my dowry have cost you?

SHYLOCK: A price I would have willingly paid.

JESSICA: The one you've now paid unwillingly is a bargain.

SHYLOCK: When your Christian has spent that so-called dowry, do you really think he'll stay with you?

JESSICA: When we married, we swore to stay together. Just like you and mother did.

SHYLOCK: Your mother was a Jew.

JESSICA: Obviously.

SHYLOCK: Therefore you are a Jew. You will always be a Jew. To your Christian and to everyone else.

JESSICA: You're saying being born a Jew is the same thing as being born black.

SHYLOCK: You know what happened right here in Venice. That black general, Othello, killed the young Venetian noble woman he married and then himself.

JESSICA: And you know some guy who pretended he was their friend figured out how to do in both of them.

SHYLOCK: What kind of friends does your husband have?

JESSICA: Real ones.

SHYLOCK: Like Antonio. The man who spits on me.

JESSICA: No one's gonna harm you. Not while I'm around.

SHYLOCK: You cannot really think you can protect me from all of them.

JESSICA: I came here to make a deal. Are you interested?

SHYLOCK: I will make no deals with you.

JESSICA: That pound of flesh you're after. You think it will make you happy. It won't.

SHYLOCK: When Leah died, my happiness was buried with her.

JESSICA: I don't only want you to take the money for Antonio's sake. I want you to do it for yours.

SHYLOCK: The court, not you, will judge what is just for me.

JESSICA: I can't believe cutting him up means that much to you.

SHYLOCK: This man has loathed and disrespected me from the moment we laid eyes on each other.

JESSICA: You chase each other for the same spice business like two crabs trapped in a bottle.

SHYLOCK: Business was not just business with him. He said it himself. It mattered most to him to defeat me because I am a Jew.

JESSICA: If you go ahead with this trial in a Christian court, you'll give him what he wants.

SHYLOCK: He wants to destroy my business.

JESSICA: He wants to get you to do something dumb. To get under your skin.

SHYLOCK: I will get under his skin.

JESSICA: Think back. Bassanio needed the money in the first place. To your great profit, he'll pay you double what Antonio owes.

SHYLOCK: Profit comes in many forms.

JESSICA: How is a pound of flesh profit?

SHYLOCK: Of course it pleases me that I take it from this vile man. But it is more.

JESSICA: Show him some mercy and you'll shame him into changing.

SHYLOCK: It won't. If I behave like a Christian and turn the other cheek, they all will mock me.

JESSICA: The way I see it, they'll respect you for getting back double the original loan.

SHYLOCK: Then look again.

JESSICA: All I see is a two hundred percent interest on that loan.

SHYLOCK: The world will call Antonio sly. Admire him for having someone else pay.

JESSICA: Grant mercy when no one expects you to. That's sly.

SHYLOCK: If Christians don't fear me, they will all behave like Antonio. I will demand my pound of flesh from him.

JESSICA: You'll only get it if a Christian court goes your way.

SHYLOCK: It will. As long these men feel guilty about charging one another interest, they need Jews. They need me.

JESSICA: You could've gotten the court wrong. Why take the chance?

SHYLOCK: They know. If the court cheats me, the others cannot expect the Jews of Venice to just shrug their shoulders and still lend them money.

JESSICA: All it takes is one person to find a weakness in your case, and you're out your money. And Antonio's fate is no longer of any value to you. Mercy is a much safer bet.

[Lights come up on father and daughter.]

FATHER: You know you really haven't set it up for Shylock to see it her way.

[Daughter smiles]

END OF SCENE 1

Scene 2

Scene: *Venetian Palace of Justice. Shylock, still in jeans and t-shirt, now wigless, wears the beaded cross necklace Jessica wore in the last scene. He sits at a table. Then ANTONIO, also in jeans and t-shirt, enters and sits across from Shylock. Lastly PORTIA enters. She is impersonating Balthasar and wears a full beard and moustache. Portia/Balthasar sits at the head of the table. Father and daughter stand to the side and watch.*

PORTIA: His grace, the duke, has appointed me to judge this criminal case.

SHYLOCK: Master Balthasar, the lawyer who spoke for the man I now prosecute. My judge. I should have guessed.

> [*Shylock starts to stand up to leave. Portia motions him to sit down.*]

PORTIA: Shylock, you above all people can have no doubt. I know the law. I will see to it that you and Antonio abide by it.

ANTONIO: Then enforce it. Jews have no right to bring criminal charges against a Christian.

> [*Shylock waves his cross at Antonio.*]

ANTONIO: By wearing that cross, you mock our religion. You are just like all those Spanish Jews who pretend to convert.

SHYLOCK: A Christian priest baptized me . He showed me how to pray the rosary. After mass, he tells me to eat a wafer he calls the body of Christ. And I swallow it.

ANTONIO: Your father was a Jew. Your mother was a Jew. In your heart, so are you.

SHYLOCK: Do you know how the Inquisition in Spain seeks to discover false converts?

ANTONIO: They put them on the rack and twist their bodies until they confess.

SHYLOCK: First they send spies to see if the converts eat pork.

ANTONIO: Shall I have my servants bring you some?

SHYLOCK: You can have my daughter's Christian lord and master come to this court and testify what he serves me when I visit his house.

ANTONIO: And how have you taken back your circumcision?

PORTIA: Enough. The court considers Shylock a Christian.

[*To Shylock*]

Now your time has come to state the charges against Antonio.

SHYLOCK: I loaned him money. He loaned that money to Bassanio. Then he charged Bassanio interest. Church and Venetian law say only Jews can charge interest on a loan. For acting like a Jew, he must be punished.

ANTONIO: I did not charge Bassanio interest.

SHYLOCK: But you did.

ANTONIO: The once and future Jew lies.

SHYLOCK: You feared losing a pound of flesh. So you had Bassanio offer me double the original loan.

ANTONIO: I borrowed that money from another Jew. What of it?

SHYLOCK: When Bassanio paid you back double the original loan, he paid you interest on that first loan.

ANTONIO: I made him a second, personal loan. He paid no interest on either.

SHYLOCK: A fiction. With the second, he paid you interest on the first.

PORTIA: Unless in making the second loan the parties cited the first, it cannot legally be called interest.

ANTONIO: Just as when I borrowed money from you, Bassanio witnessed this agreement as well.

SHYLOCK:

[*To Portia*]

Is only his word enough?

ANTONIO:

[*To Portia*]

Bring Bassanio to court. Put him under oath. He will tell you.

PORTIA:

[*Calling off stage.*]

Pursuivant! Fetch Bassanio.

[*To Shylock and Antonio.*]

We will adjourn the court until he arrives.

SHYLOCK: But I have another charge.

ANTONIO: No doubt as false as the first.

PORTIA: Then make your charge.

SHYLOCK: In contravention of the laws of Venice and of the Holy Church, this man has committed abominations.

PORTIA: Name them.

SHYLOCK: In the Christian Bible it says, "If a man lies with a man as with a woman, both have committed an abomination. They shall surely be put to death; their blood is upon them." Antonio has used men as though they were women.

ANTONIO: You have no proof.

SHYLOCK: At your request, my proof will soon arrive.

PORTIA: Bassanio?

SHYLOCK: Bassanio.

PORTIA: Are you saying my hus...

> [*Catches herself before she can say Bassanio is her husband.*]

Are you saying Bassanio lay with Antonio?

SHYLOCK: The first loan cost 3000 ducats. The interest, another 3000.

PORTIA: The sum is not in dispute. Why bring it up?

SHYLOCK: This man knew. If he failed to repay, he would forfeit a pound of flesh. And perhaps his life. No one does such a thing without expecting a greatly desired reward in return.

FATHER: All right.

> [*Lights come up on father and daughter.*]

You're just checking boxes.

DAUGHTER: What boxes?

FATHER: You got lucky because Shakespeare already checked one for you. Portia is not only Bassanio's wife, but she's in drag as Balthasar. One box checked. If Antonio is gay, of course that means Bassanio is bi. Two boxes checked in one go.

DAUGHTER: Any more boxes on your mind?

FATHER: I think I've made my point. You just go along with your crowd.

DAUGHTER: I'd like some people in the audience who aren't collecting Social Security.

FATHER: So, like I said, to get them, you checked the boxes.

DAUGHTER: Name me an era when no one checked boxes. Shakespeare had only men as actors to please his audience. Then they wanted happy endings. Next moustache twirling villains getting their comeuppance. Even when you started acting, blond virgin heroines. Whores with hearts of gold.

FATHER: I didn't care much for those efforts at pandering either.

DAUGHTER: But you and everyone else did it. To keep critics off your back. To fill those seats. If I don't show the audience characters that match their values, I won't have an audience.

FATHER: Like I said, you're box checking.

DAUGHTER: It seems to me that there are a variety of ways to check boxes.

FATHER: A checked box is a checked box.

DAUGHTER: I don't think it's that simple. Isn't the key to a good play no square pegs, round holes? For my audience, a gay Antonio's a round, not a square, peg.

FATHER: And you've made very clear where the round hole is located.

[*To the actors*]

Play on.

PORTIA: I know Bassanio as well as one human being can know another. He would not do such a thing.

SHYLOCK: When he arrives, by your command, he will be put under oath. If he lies, his faith tells him his immortal soul will roast for all eternity in the fires of Hell. We shall see.

PORTIA: He will not answer. If he says what you claim, he would forfeit his life.

SHYLOCK: Even if he refuses, he confirms this merchant's guilt.

PORTIA:

[*Calling off stage.*]

Send a messenger to recall the pursuivant!

SHYLOCK: So I shall receive no justice.

PORTIA: On the contrary. You made your point. It does not matter what Bassanio will say. Antonio stand.

[*He does.*]

Antonio, there may come a time when what you evidently did will cease to violate the law. Unfortunately, now you must be condemned of violating that law.

[*Portia starts to say something, then stops.*]

SHYLOCK: In the first trial, you found a clever way to prevent shedding this man's blood. Now, uphold the law. Shed it.

PORTIA: If the laws of God and Venice are strictly enforced, that is the penalty.

SHYLOCK: I note the word "strictly."

PORTIA: I know the last time you showed no mercy. Now that you are a Christian, is there any?

SHYLOCK: I want justice done. Always.

ANTONIO: You mean, Jew, get your revenge.

SHYLOCK: Many in this world no longer considers me a Jew.

ANTONIO: I will never consider you a Christian.

SHYLOCK: What if I act as a Christian?

ANTONIO: And how would you do that?

SHYLOCK: By having this court offer you an alternative punishment.

PORTIA: Name it.

SHYLOCK: Just as I was sentenced to become a Christian, I would have this man sentenced to become a Jew.

ANTONIO: This is your version of Christian mercy.

SHYLOCK: It would be fitting.

ANTONIO: A Jew's eye for an eye.

SHYLOCK: Fitting. The Church says only Jews may charge interest. That they commit abominations. You are already a Jew. The court should confirm it and have you circumcised.

ANTONIO: Then for me death would be the only true Christian mercy.

PORTIA: In the name of mercy, that is your sentence.

[*Lights come up on father and daughter.*]

DAUGHTER: Well?

FATHER: I didn't think you could do it. But you did.

DAUGHTER: I'm almost afraid to ask what the "it" is.

FATHER: Strained the quality of mercy.

THE END

GOOD DEEDS

CHARACTERS:

Salka
Berthold
Louis B. Mayer
Ben
Ernst
Terry
State Department Official

Act 1,
Scene 1

Scene: *SALKA VIERTEL and ERNST sit at her kitchen table in Klosters, Switzerland. Salka is a gray haired woman in her late sixties. She wears plain clothing, but has an expensive bright blue silk scarf around her neck. Ernst, his early fifties, is also dressed plainly. A teapot and the remains of a small chocolate cake sit on the table between them. A couple of tea cups and small cake plates are also on the table. On a wall facing the audience there is a large calendar. It has a picture of the Statue of Liberty on it with the year 1956 in large numerals written across the top.*

SALKA: Ernst, Ernst, Ernst. I'll say it again. I'm so glad you could visit. So glad.

> *(Salka reaches across the table, takes Ernst's hand in both of hers and gently squeezes them. He takes one of her hands and kisses it.)*

ERNST: Even on the other side of the ocean. Compliments in American English.

SALKA: You just managed to double my pleasure.

ERNST: How?

SALKA: By coming to see me. And by speaking to me in a language you'd like to forget.

ERNST: Now Salka, I don't want you to think I have become sentimental. I came for your chocolate cake.

SALKA:

> *(Smiles and shakes her head.)*

Of course you did.

ERNST: I remember your cake. And your guests. I loved listening to your guests.

SALKA: You added glamor and wit to our gatherings.

ERNST: Brecht had more glamor than three of me. But it's kind of you to say so.

SALKA: There's something about exiles getting together. It brings out our best.

ERNST: I hope that isn't why you now have become one.

SALKA: I think you know me better than that.

ERNST: You have always been so proud of becoming an American.

SALKA: Not the worst of my sins.

ERNST: Yet here you are in your Swiss apartment. Truly ironic.

SALKA: Ernst, I'm sure you noticed. The world is filled with irony.

ERNST: Your piece of the world now has its share.

SALKA: Two wandering Jews with our positions reversed. That is truly ironic.

ERNST: I have stopped wandering.

SALKA : But these days, you're the one who wants to help take care of me.

ERNST: There is an Americanism. Something like, what goes around should come back.

SALKA: And you think it applies to me.

ERNST: You know it does.

SALKA: I'll put it another way. We all ride this carousel.

ERNST: So many good deeds. You deserved better than a carousel ride back to where you started.

END OF SCENE 1

Scene 2

Scene: *Study in the Viertel house. BERTHOLD sits behind a desk cluttered with ledgers and an adding machine. He has cleared a space and writes on a pad in that space. Salka, looking much younger than in Scene 1, arranges a large bunch of unsorted flowers with a pruning sheers and puts them vases.*

BERTHOLD: Really. The man who can fire you.

> (*Salka stops arranging the flowers, shrugs her shoulders and blows Berthold a kiss.*
>
> *Berthold then pretends to catch it and rub it on his lips. When he blows a kiss back, Salka pretends to do the same.*)

Dearest heart. You could be the bravest person I know.

SALKA: My darling Berthold, after twenty years together, if you wish me to join you in the bedroom, just ask. No flattery needed.

BERTHOLD: But it's true. And you're trying to change the subject.

SALKA: So what brings on this compliment?

BERTHOLD: You. Running the danger Mayer will take offense. He could bid you a not so fond farewell.

SALKA: He asked me to come to his office for a gin game. That is the time to ask him.

BERTHOLD: You don't really believe he's only asked you to his office to play cards.

SALKA: Of course not. He probably wants a favor. What better time to twist his arm. A bit.

BERTHOLD: So when you metaphorically twist his arm to help Jews get over here. He will say, "Thank you. Please twist some more."

SALKA: I also think he won't say, Stop! Shut up! In the end, he'll help bring the Jews here.

BERTHOLD: You want this favor from the man who would like everyone to forget he's a Jew.

SALKA: Like us, he prefers not to continually make a point of it.

BERTHOLD: We don't go out of our way to be photographed with Cardinal Spellman.

SALKA: He noticed that Catholics can go to his movies too.

BERTHOLD: My dearest heart. I must confess I don't understand you.

SALKA: So, I am your woman of mystery.

BERTHOLD: Your best friend is Garbo, an a-political Swedish Christian.

SALKA: Obviously.

BERTHOLD: At our weekly open house, it is difficult to think of a country or a religion that isn't represented.

SALKA: Including Jews.

BERTHOLD:

(*A little wistfully*)

Including German Jews who both delight me and make me homesick.

SALKA: You should be pleased. I want to add more of them to the mix.

BERTHOLD: If you could do it without endangering your career, I would cheer you on.

SALKA: You'll see, my darling Berthold. You will have reason to cheer.

BERTHOLD:

(*Looking and sounding puzzled*)

My heart, I hope you don't feel the need to work off that totally undeserved sense of Jewish guilt.

(*Pause*)

Or maybe your Jewish mother instincts have overwhelmed you.

> (*Salka blows Berthold another kiss and goes on arranging the flowers.*)

END OF SCENE 2

Scene 3

Scene: *LOUIS B MAYER's lavish office - deep pile rug, bookcases filled with books and Oscars, plush sofa, huge oak desk and a chair behind it that could be mistaken for a padded throne. There is a large autographed picture of Herbert Hoover hanging on a back wall and an equally large calender with 1938 in large numerals on the top. A drinks cart and glasses are at the side of the desk.*

    Salka and Mayer enter and sit center stage at a card table. Salka dresses expensively and wears the same scarf she did in scene 1. She deals cards and puts the deck down in the center of the table.

MAYER: Drink Salka?

                  (Nods in the direction of a drinks cart)

Help yourself.

                  (Salka puts her cards down, gets up and starts to walk toward the drinks cart. She glances at Mayer who is trying, ineffectively, to look nonchalant. She goes back to the table, picks up her cards and then gets herself a drink and returns to her seat. Mayer looks disappointed.)

SALKA: Are we playing for money or fun?

MAYER: We need to talk.

SALKA: About?

MAYER: About money. Big money.

(Mayer and Salka play gin rummy as they talk.)

SALKA: So let's talk.

MAYER: Garbo's next movie.

> (*Salka finishes his sentence.*)

SALKA: Queen Christina.

MAYER: Yeah. You gotta rework the script or it'll cost me a pile.

SALKA: Garbo's movies make you a pile. A big pile. She loves this script.

MAYER: Yeah, yeah.

SALKA: So what's the problem?

MAYER: Gotta change it anyway.

SALKA: The censors.

MAYER: What about 'em?

SALKA: You let the boys with the red pencils get at it.

> (*When Mayer discards a card, Salka picks it up.*)

MAYER: You don't know what talkin' you're about.

SALKA: Mr. Mayer, do I look dumb?

> (*Mayer discards again and Salka picks up again.*)

MAYER: They ain't censoring nothing.

SALKA: He says with a straight face.

MAYER: They're tellin' me how to make money.

SALKA: Come on.

MAYER: Look. The people that don't like seein' sex or politics in their movies. These guys know what they like to see.

SALKA: To make money in Nazi Germany I suppose you let Hitler's boys go over my script.

MAYER: So what if I do.

SALKA: I can't believe I need to tell another Jew "so what".

MAYER: Some guy here at the German consulate.

SALKA: You really sent him my script.

MAYER: He didn't ask who wrote it. I didn't tell him.

SALKA: So now I'm writing Nazi propaganda.

MAYER: Well, you got an Aryan queen gettin' the better of everyone, don't you?

SALKA: It's history. I didn't make it up for some Nazi's stamp of approval.

MAYER: The queen-woman part didn't thrill him, but the Aryan part did.

SALKA: Oy veys mir.

MAYER: Save it for temple.

SALKA: It's got to bother you at least a little bit. Having some Nazi look over your shoulder.

MAYER: Of course it bothers me.

SALKA: But not that much.

MAYER: You think I don't know. If I lived over there, those Nazi bastards would take away all my money. Then they'd throw me out.

SALKA: Good job you landed here when you did. Good job both of us did.

MAYER: Finally. Somethin' we ain't gonna fight about.

SALKA:

> (*Trying, but failing, to sound nonchalant*)

If there was a way for more Jews to get out of Germany now, would you go for it?

MAYER:

> (*Mayer discards slowly from his hand and takes from the deck as deliberately during his line.*)

Depends.

SALKA:

> (*Salka discards and picks Mayer's discard up quickly.*)

Think sponsors.

MAYER: Okay. I'm thinkin'.

SALKA: You sponsored me and Berthold.

MAYER: Way back when.

SALKA: Time to pick up where you left off.

> (*Mayer picks up one of Salka's discards.*)

MAYER: Now you want me to sponsor all the Jews in Germany. You're just kiddin' me.

SALKA: I save my jokes for the scripts.

MAYER: Even if I wanted to, I ain't rich enough...

> (*Salka cuts him off.*)

SALKA: Lots of big-wigs look up to you.

MAYER: Or pretend to.

SALKA: Put out the word.

MAYER:

> (*Sarcastically*)

Yeah, I'll take out a full-page ad in the Hollywood Reporter.

SALKA: You could.

MAYER: And let that Nazi putz who looks at the scripts know what I'm up to.

SALKA: You could say something to the people at your golf club.

MAYER: You and your husband can do that.

SALKA: People who matter respect you a hell of a lot more than us.

MAYER: You should figure out a way to hide the buttering up.

SALKA: What if I appeal to your profit margin?

MAYER: You better. So far you just got me doin' a lot of extra work. For free.

SALKA: How about this. You get sponsors to bring over people who can work for you.

MAYER: Suppose they don't wanna work for me.

SALKA: Turn on the charm. Jack Warner doesn't have any.

MAYER: I don't get why you're doin' this.

SALKA: Things are getting really nasty there.

MAYER: Look around. Us Jews ain't exactly popular here.

SALKA: Are you saying Nazi Germany and the U.S. are the same?

MAYER: I bet you seen the pictures of that flyboy hero, Lindberg, shakin' hands with Hitler.

SALKA: Living here still beats living there.

MAYER: If Jews keep runnin' away every time there's a pogrom, they're gonna be runnin' forever.

SALKA: Running here would be good.

MAYER: So now you want to change how the world works.

SALKA: I want you to help take a little piece of it. The Jewish piece. Make it better.

MAYER: Let me think on it.

SALKA:

> (*Salka picks up a Meyer discard and then lays here cards on the table.*)

Gin.

MAYER: Just a friendly game right?

> (*Salka smiles.*)

END OF SCENE 3

Scene 4

Scene: *Louis B. Mayer's office. Mayer is dressed to play golf. So is BEN. Both their golf bags stand upright near the office door.*

MAYER: Studio commissary's still open, Ben. I could have 'em send up sandwiches.

BEN: My deli or nothin'.

MAYER: Here ain't bad.

BEN: How long that chauffeur of yours gonna be?

MAYER: Now you're in a rush.

BEN: I promised to get Salka her order.

MAYER: I don't get the in person treatment.

BEN: You don't give me a slice of Salka's chocolate cake.

MAYER: So?

BEN: I ain't gonna let no delivery guy get my piece.

MAYER: By the way, Salka wanted me talk to you about this scheme of hers.

BEN: What scheme?

MAYER: Sponsorin' Jews to get 'em over here before Hitler does 'em in.

BEN: Let me guess. She wants me to be a sponsor.

MAYER: You and lots of others.

BEN: Enough of us Jews here already.

MAYER: A few more don't hurt.

BEN: Maybe one day the goys 'll start eatin' bagel with a schmear. But they ain't gonna ask us to join 'em.

MAYER: And the goys are so good at figurin' out who's Jewish.

BEN: You know what's goin' on here. Gotta keep are heads down. Stirrin' things up ain't a good idea.

MAYER: So just advertise your deli on the radio.

BEN: All of us 'll get it in the neck anyway.

MAYER: So tell me why.

BEN: A bunch of Jews that don't speak English so good stick out.

MAYER: So you and me don't sound like Shakespeare.

BEN: I tell yah. They'll make it worse for us.

MAYER: No one's askin' any of 'em to run for president. Just t' work.

BEN: The goyum think we already got Franklin Delano Rosenvelt.

MAYER: You been hangin' out with my comedy writers for too long.

BEN: Serious now. Where they gonna work?

MAYER: Maybe at your deli. So I don't have t' wait till a week from Tuesday for a corned beef sandwich.

BEN: You think we can just say "poof" and food 'll appear.

MAYER: So hire piano players. Then I don't notice how long I gotta sit there.

(*Ben looks a Mayer and makes a wry* face.)

BEN: Them piano players and the rest of 'em. I hear they're just a bunch of Commies.

MAYER:

(*For a moment Mayer looks thoughtful. Then he brightens up.*)

I sponsored Salka and her husband. They ain't Commies.

BEN:

                    (*Waves toward the picture of Herbert Hoover.*)

You just wanted to get 'em over here in time so they could vote for Lincoln.

MAYER: You willin' to risk never eatin' Salka's chocolate cake?

BEN: I don't know.

MAYER: Look. When you deliver the stuff to Salka's, talk to her about it.

END OF SCENE 4

Scene 5

Scene: *Viertel living room. Salka gets ready for company, stacking plates and silverware on a table. She rearranges flowers. An uncut chocolate cake lies at the far end of the table. There is a knock at the door.*

SALKA: Ben? Is that you?

> (*Without waiting for a reply then says:*)

Come in, come in.

> (*Still dressed in his golfing outfit, Ben enters carrying food trays that he puts on the table and begins to arrange them, edging closer to the chocolate cake as he works.*)

BEN: Louis don't like to rush his golf game when he's losin'. Sorry.

SALKA: Let me guess. He lost a bet too.

> (*Ben stops working for a minute, pulls some paper money out of his pocket, waves it in Salka's direction, chuckles to himself, and goes back to arranging the food on the table.*)

SALKA: Nice to see you have money to wave around. That reminds me...

> (*Ben interrupts.*)

BEN: Louis warned me about you and your meshuggah ideas.

SALKA: Getting Jews away from Hitler isn't crazy.

BEN: We got Nazis marchin' all around here. They wanna throw us out. Or lock us up. You're gonna make it worse.

SALKA: Ben, hiding in a hole won't stop the Nazis.

BEN: And you think bringin' more Jews over here will.

SALKA: Show that bunch of thugs they can't frighten you.

BEN: You talk like they don't frighten you.

SALKA: Let's scare them for a change.

BEN: You're tellin' me bringin' more Jews is gonna have 'em shakin' in their boots.

SALKA: As long as we're alive, they lose.

BEN: We'll stay that way, if we don't do nothin' dumb.

SALKA: Ben, I bet you give money at your temple to help Jewish refugees.

BEN: Yeah. So?

SALKA: So you're already giving the Nazis a hard time. Help bring some over. Give Hitler a little harder time.

BEN: It's like puttin' ketchup on sieg heil bunch's corned beef. Just makes 'em mad.

SALKA : I hope so.

BEN: It ain't your plate glass window they're gonna smash.

SALKA: Ben. You own a Jewish deli. If they want to smash windows, your place is already on their list.

BEN: Even if my windows stays whole, I told Louis. I don't got money to hire 'em.

SALKA: Do you want to know why he still wants you to sponsor someone?

BEN: Yeah.

SALKA: Your golfing buddy wants to hire a lot of them. Cheap.

BEN:
> (*Ben's face shows he gets it.*)

Okay. Okay. Suppose, just suppose, I was to sponsor somebody.

(Salka can't contain her enthusiasm and gives Ben a kiss on the cheek. He looks sheepish and then serious.)

BEN: How do I know I ain't gonna end up with some deadbeat who runs up a buncha bills I gotta pay.

SALKA: The U.S. government. They're looking for excuses to kick Jews back to the place Hitler runs.

BEN: Then how do I know I'm not backin' some Commie who's just lookin' for a chance to slit my throat?

SALKA: We'll bring over people who compose music, play the piano, sing love songs. They don't sound like throat-slitters to me.

BEN: All right already. Yah wore me down.

SALKA: Great!

BEN: Just one more thing to seal the deal.

SALKA: Name it.

BEN: When I'm done here. I get the whole chocolate cake. Not just a slice.

END OF SCENE 5

Scene 6

Scene: *Ernst looks much younger than he did in the first scene. He is in the final stages of gathering up his belongings in his Paris apartment. His well used suitcase is on the floor and he moves a trumpet out of the way so he can pack it more easily.*

TERRY, an African American, sits up in a double bed with a blanket covering the lower half of his body. In the distance air raid sirens wail.

ERNST: You should come with me.

TERRY: I did. It was lovely.

ERNST:

> *(For a moment, he looks puzzled and then serious.)*

This is not a time for humor.

TERRY: If I don't laugh, I'll cry.

ERNST:

> *(Ernst stops packing for a moment and then continues.)*

I have no choice.

TERRY: I don't want to sound like someone in one of those afternoon radio dramas. But I'd give anything if we could stay here together.

ERNST: The Nazis are on their way here to Paris. In tanks.

TERRY: The French army'll hold them.

ERNST: Spoken like an American who knows nothing of the French Army. Or the Nazi one. Come with me.

TERRY: Where could we go?

ERNST: Out of Paris. Out of France. Maybe to America.

TERRY: I'm not going back to some ghetto.

ERNST: And I will not stay put so the Nazis can put me in one. Or some place worse.

TERRY: The French treat me like a human being. You too.

ERNST: But that is my point. The Nazis will not.

TERRY: Let's take the worst thing that can happen. The French lose the war.

(*Ernst interrupts.*)

ERNST: And the Nazis will hunt us both down.

TERRY: They'll have a million things to do here. Just keep your head low.

ERNST: The scars you wondered about on my back. They came from fighting the Nazis on the Berlin streets. Believe me. They will see to it that, as you Americans put it, we are handed our heads.

TERRY: I'm not going back.

ERNST: I wish I could.

> (*Ernst takes his suitcase and exits. Lights dim. The sound of running footsteps. Off stage voice says:*)

Halt! Halt! Oder Ich schiesse!

> (*Three gun shots*)

END OF SCENE 6

Scene 7

Scene: *On the balcony of Salka's house in Santa Monica, Ernst sits perched on a low railing. He's dressed neatly, but plainly in a suit jacket, white shirt, tie, slacks and shoes that tie.*

Above the door to the balcony is a big sign reading "Roosevelt Wins #3. Hooray!" Ocean sounds come from the front of the stage. Ernst looks pensively in the direction of the sound of the breaking waves. From the back of the stage, the noise from a party, muffled by the closed French doors, filters onto the balcony.

When the doors open, the noise grows louder. Salka comes through them to the balcony. She has on an expensive party dress. As she closes the doors behind her, the sound becomes muted again. Over the course of the first lines, the sounds of the ocean and those of the party fade out.

SALKA: An irresistible view, isn't it?

ERNST: I find it disconcerting.

SALKA: Disconcerting? Such a word. Impressive.

ERNST: The product of a misspent youth among American musicians in Berlin and Paris.

SALKA: Then America isn't quite the shock for you that it is for some of the other exiles.

ERNST: But it is. I went from big city to big city.

(*Pronouncing the town very carefully*)

San-ta Mon-ic-a with its ocean sounds seems very strange.

SALKA: The seacoast of Hollywood.

ERNST: Do you know what feels even stranger? Hearing dozens people on a palm tree lined beach, talking German.

SALKA: But that's how we Jews started out. Living among the palms with the Mediterranean waves in the background.

ERNST: As Moses and his people roamed the desert, I think their German was something short of conversational.

SALKA: Surely you've figured out that Jews, even German Jews, are liable to turn up anywhere.

ERNST: That you helped bring so many of us here I find even stranger.

SALKA: Hollywood. The new Jerusalem. All we have to do is hang on.

ERNST: Too much. Too much.

SALKA: Why do you say that?

ERNST: I've always considered myself a German first.

SALKA: And then a Jew?

ERNST: And then a Communist who wants to save the world.

SALKA: Despite the fact Stalin and his new friend, Hitler, destroy it country by country.

ERNST:

(*Harshly*)

Stalin is no Communist. He is an ex-priest who runs Russia. He starved the Ukrainians to death. Everywhere he slaughters the true Communists.

SALKA: If you don't want Stalin, I take it you have someone else in mind.

ERNST: On my travels here I stopped in Mexico City. Music lover that he is, Trotsky was kind enough to invite me to his house. A very impressive man.

SALKA: Oh, you prefer a Jewish Communist.

ERNST: Trotsky is no more a Jew than I am.

SALKA: But there is a Jewish part. In both of you.

ERNST: If I made a list of what makes me a human being, the Jewish part would not rank very high.

SALKA: You know better than most. In places the Nazis occupy, they make that list.

ERNST: And here?

SALKA: I'll give you a lawyer's answer. It depends.

ERNST: American lawyers and their "on the one hand" answers. It has brought them world-wide fame.

SALKA:

> (*Smiling, as Salka speaks, she briefly extends a hand.*)

On the one hand, Hitler has his admirers among the palms.

ERNST: There is, I presume, another hand.

SALKA: They're noisy, not influential.

ERNST: In Berlin they were just noisy. Until they were more than that.

SALKA: We fight them every way we can.

ERNST: You mean you buy guns.

SALKA: No, no. We're writers, artists, musicians. Like you.

ERNST: I fought them in the streets. For all the good it did.

SALKA: We write. We perform.

ERNST: I am sorry to say this, but that just makes the people who do it feel good.

SALKA: It does make us feel good. But it isn't useless. Our benefits raise money for exiles.

ERNST: You cannot support me and the others forever.

SALKA: No, of course not. But that's why we bring you to Hollywood.

ERNST: Ah, yes. Hollywood the home of rich capitalists.

SALKA: They're mostly Jews, you know.

ERNST: I hope you understand why I find that depressing.

SALKA: The people who run the studios will pay for your talent.

ERNST: Surely not for my ballet.

SALKA: No, but they'll pay you well to write movie music.

ERNST: I know nothing about that kind of music.

SALKA: You can learn.

ERNST: I want to know nothing about that kind of music. Or them.

SALKA: I would like to dig up just a little pragmatism in you.

ERNST: To protect my life and my ideals, I left behind someone who meant much to me.

SALKA: If it makes you feel any better about being here, I'll tell you that the man who acts as your sponsor doesn't run a movie studio.

ERNST: I take it he does not run a soup kitchen for the poor either.

SALKA: Not exactly. But he does make really good corned beef sandwiches.

ERNST: Then I guess I must thank you and him for your good will and go on my travels again.

SALKA: Stay. You could do so much.

ERNST: I would like to ask you what may seem like a rude question.

SALKA: Ask.

ERNST: Why do you care such a great deal what happens to me?

SALKA: Not just you.

ERNST: Then to all us. I am curious.

SALKA: My dear husband, Berthold, thinks it's to work off my in-born Jewish guilt. And maternal instincts.

ERNST: I take it he is not right.

SALKA: He's such a dear, dear lost man.

ERNST: I trust you do not expect me to guess.

SALKA: No. I'll tell you. The Nazis behave as though we Jews aren't human beings. But we are. So I help save lives however I can.

ERNST: As the Communist who wants to save all of humanity, I understand.

SALKA: I don't think I can save all of it. Just the limited number I can reach.

> [*Salka reaches out with both her hands and takes Ernst's.*]

END OF SCENE 7

Scene 8

Scene: *Salka leaves Ernst and walks back through the balcony doors. The party noises have stopped. She sees Berthold cleaning up the living room. He finds the remains of the chocolate cake and gobbles it up. Salka looks at him and smiles. He grins back and goes on cleaning up.*

SALKA: In making your rounds among our guests this evening, did you hear anything interesting?

BERTHOLD: I heard some intelligent German spoken. Or maybe I should say I heard some intelligent Germans speaking.

> *(Berthold licks the last of the chocolate frosting from his fingers and Salka wags her forefinger at him.)*

SALKA: Speaking of intelligent German speakers, by any chance, did you encounter Ernst,

> *(Nods back toward the balcony.)*

my newly arrived composer?

BERTHOLD:

> *(Goes over and looks out the glass patio doors.)*

Your young man looks like an abandoned puppy walking on a sandy beach for the first time.

SALKA: I would like to make him into a fully grown hound. Ready for the hunt.

> *(Berthold stops what he is doing and thinks about possibilities.)*

BERTHOLD: I have an idea that might stimulate growth. But he'd have to go to New York.

SALKA:

> (*Goes over to Berthold and kisses him on the cheek.*)

The next sound you now hear will be Ernst jumping for joy.

BERTHOLD: The jumping. How appropriate. I have in mind that choreographer, Jerome Robbins.

SALKA: Jerome Robbins. I've heard his name from somewhere. Do you know him?

BERTHOLD: I know theater people who do. And they are impressed. From what I hear, Robbins and your Ernst are very much alike.

SALKA: That would be nice.

BERTHOLD: Robbins believes in using modern music for dance.

SALKA: Promising.

BERTHOLD: And I hear he belonged to the Communist party, but then dropped out.

SALKA: If it wasn't such a bad pun, I'd be tempted to say that will be music to Ernst's ears.

BERTHOLD:

> (*Grimaces and then smiles.*)

And, from what I observe of your most recent protégée, like Robbins, young women are seldom his first choice as companions.

SALKA: It's almost like some kind of god designed the two of them for one another.

BERTHOLD: Since they are non-observant Jews, hopefully not a vengeful, Jewish one.

SALKA: Seems unlikely, doesn't it.

END OF ACT I

Act 2,
Scene 1

Scene: *Louis B. Mayer's office at MGM. The oversized calendar on the back wall shows 1940. The card table is gone. So is the picture of Herbert Hoover. Mayer stands with golf putter, putting golf balls toward an artificial golf course hole. Because the deep pile of the rug makes the golf balls roll slowly, he stands near the side of his desk the down stage, only a foot or two away from the hole. There is a knock at the door.*

MAYER: Come in Salka.

> (*Salka enters. Mayer looks up and goes back to putting without much success. Concentrating of his golf, he motions Salka to sit on the sofa. Instead, Salka finds a chair and puts it in front of Mayer's desk, facing him. He gives Salka an exasperated look and continues putting.*)

MAYER: Garbo. We need to talk. Again.

SALKA: So let's talk.

MAYER: You gotta tell her to behave.

SALKA: You're her boss.

MAYER: She don't listen to me.

SALKA: Tell me what you mean by, behave.

MAYER: Some day soon I want her to pick a movie to shoot.

SALKA: You know her contract says it's her choice.

MAYER: Tell her to pick one.

SALKA: We both know I'd never do that.

MAYER: She ain't the star she used to be.

SALKA: But she still has a contract.

MAYER: For one more movie. She keeps this up, it'll be her last movie.

SALKA: I'll take that back to her and see what she says.

MAYER: Look, Salka, I like you.

SALKA: Good to know.

MAYER: Before Garbo goes, get to know Heddy Lamarr.

SALKA: I take it you think we'd make a good fit.

MAYER: A nice Jewish girl with a Catholic mother. From Vienna. Make her fit. Your favorite shiksa's on her way out.

> (*At last Mayer gets one of his golf balls in the*
> *hole. A look of satisfaction spreads on his face.*)

END OF SCENE 1

Scene 2

Scene: *The study in Salka's house. On one wall there is a large calendar with President Roosevelt's picture on it. On top is March 1941 in large numerals. There are ledgers open on the desk. Salka, dressed informally, sits behind it. She punches numbers into a calculating machine and examines the paper tapes that come out.*

Berthold, dressed for travel, enters carrying a suitcase and puts it down. He comes up behind Salka, kisses her on the top of her head. Then squints at the ledger she has open on the desk.

BERTHOLD: Dear heart, I'm glad you're willing to try to get things under control.

SALKA: With all we're doing...

(Berthold interrupts.)

BERTHOLD: With all you are doing. I need to bring in money again.

SALKA: I know you don't like me to keep saying it.

BERTHOLD: Then don't.

SALKA: But I will. Please. No dodging Nazi U-boats in the ocean and their bombs in London.

BERTHOLD: I will tell you what drives me away.

SALKA: Hopefully not a wife who wants you to stay safe.

BERTHOLD: Hollywood's endless stream of home-grown Jewish philistines. To wit, the latest absurdity.

(Berthold takes a cigar out of his inside jacket pocket, plants it in his mouth, wiggles it and his eyebrows at the same time, imitating Groucho Marx.)

BERTHOLD: Some young man from MGM's marketing department asked me if Groucho Marx was Karl's son.

SALKA: He could've been joking.

BERTHOLD:

(*Now looking serious.*)

I can't deal with those ignorant peasants any more.

SALKA: Careful Berthold.

BERTHOLD: Well, it's true.

SALKA: Degrading names for those favored by the powers-that-be. They could have their cost.

BERTHOLD: Only if I need their money.

SALKA: Tell me. Truly. How realistic is it for you to do without their money?

BERTHOLD: More realistic than pretending MGM plans to keep paying you some paltry sum for Garbo scripts. If there are any more.

SALKA: It's not paltry.

BERTHOLD: My love. You have so many foundlings. It's no longer enough.

(*Salka takes Berthold's hand and kisses it.*)

SALKA: When the Nazis stop, I'll stop.

BERTHOLD: My heart. I fear for what will become of you before then.

SALKA: Dear, dear Berthold. You worry too much about me.

BERTHOLD: Shall I tell you what worries me?

SALKA: Please.

BERTHOLD: That if I stay here any longer with nothing to do, I will make you unhappy.

SALKA: Of course you won't.

BERTHOLD: Besides, I'm an old man and you're not an old woman.

SALKA: You're not so old and I'm not so young.

BERTHOLD: Your best years. Spent looking after me. It would be sad. So sad.

SALKA: We've always looked after each other.

> (*Berthold kisses Salka on the cheek, picks up his baggage and exits.*)

END OF SCENE 2

Scene 3

Scene: *Lights come up on stage right where Salka sits at her desk on the phone. The ledgers still piled high.*

Lights then come up stage left on Ernst, also on the phone. He sits at a desk only slightly less cluttered than Salka's, but with handwritten musical scores. A piano, with a score on the piano's built-in music stand sits in the background. On the wall Ernst has a large picture of Trotsky and a large calendar for the year 1942.

SALKA: You didn't call collect. I take it things are going well.

ERNST: Yes and No. That's why I called.

SALKA: I'm listening.

ERNST:

> (*Blurts out the first sentence quickly, then the next slowly.*)

Now that America's in the war, I want to fight the Nazis again. But for me it's complicated.

SALKA: Why?

ERNST: I tried to volunteer for the army, but I couldn't pass the physical.

SALKA: Maybe it's just as well. They could send you anywhere.

ERNST: I appealed to my local draft board. You know the local men who select soldiers. With my German, I thought the army could use me as a translator.

SALKA: And?

ERNST: They wanted to know why a German wants to join the U.S. army.

SALKA: I take it you told them you're Jewish.

ERNST: I did. Reluctantly. It made matters worse.

SALKA: Unbelievable.

ERNST: A board member said, now that "us Yanks" had to "wup" the Germans, he wasn't going to let some "God damn" Jew rub America's nose in it.

SALKA: Unpleasant encounter for you, I'm sure.

ERNST: Part of me felt relieved.

SALKA: Now I am totally confused.

ERNST: The way that man feels about helping Jews. That's the way I feel about helping that butcher, Stalin.

SALKA: Even when he's finally fighting Nazis.

ERNST: Yes. Especially since one of his assassins stuck an ice ax into Trotsky's head.

SALKA: Stalin and the Soviets are our friends. For the time being. At least now they're fighting Hitler too.

ERNST: You're right, of course. But everyone between Moscow and Berlin will pay Stalin's price.

SALKA: I hate to say it. It's the price for getting rid of the Nazis.

ERNST: I have no idea what to do.

SALKA: Show the Nazis they can't win any way you can.

ERNST: I am still a Communist at heart. As things stand, a reluctant pacifist Communist.

SALKA: Leave the shooting to others. Find a way to help the refugees over here. They need translators too.

ERNST: Of course! The other refugees. I should have thought of that.

SALKA: The good thing is, now you have.

ERNST: I will talk with Terry. See if he can help me find a New York aid group.

SALKA: Choose the group carefully.

ERNST: What do you mean, carefully?

SALKA: I belonged to one of those groups. Then I found out Stalin's Communists ran it. Badly. I got out.

ERNST: Stalin follows everywhere.

SALKA: After we win the war, you'll be one of the few people here who cares.

END OF SCENE 3

Scene 4

Scene: *Ernst's apartment. Everything is the same as the previous scene except for the calendar that now says 1950. Ernst works on writing down a musical score while the radio plays a news program.*

(*Voice from the radio.*)

H.B. Kaltenborn here with the national news. The House Un-American Activities Committee continued its hearings about Communist influence on Broadway. They struck gold with today's witness, Jerome Robbins, one of the Great White Way's most prominent and promising young men. He spent a great deal of time in the witness chair naming Communists. He singled out the immigrant composer, Ernst Stern, for particular attention.

(*Ernst stops working on his score, turns toward the radio. He looks stunned.*)

This reporter saw an FBI agent I know taking careful notes. I certainly would not want to be one of the people Robbins named. Especially not Mr. Stern.

(*Lights dim and come up and a table in a café. Ernst sits facing Terry. Terry speaks nervously and periodically looks around him. He silently motions Ernst to leave the table at which they sit and go to another, more isolated one.*)

TERRY: Yesterday. While you were gone. I had visitors I didn't want.

ERNST: The FBI, I presume.

TERRY: They flashed badges and shoved their way in.

ERNST: But you are not a Communist.

TERRY: They wanted to know about you.

ERNST: I guess I should expect them back at our door soon.

TERRY: Maybe not that soon.

ERNST: Why do you say that?

TERRY: They're working their way down a list of men.

(*Ernst cuts in.*)

ERNST: What men?

TERRY: A list of men we know. At the Stonewall Inn.

ERNST: I don't understand. What we do is not illegal.

TERRY: I heard they threatened Robbins. Told him they'd put his homosexual sex life all over the newspapers. Ruin his reputation.

ERNST: I guess that is why he did that carefully choreographed dance in front of the committee.

(*Pause*)

I think I'd better phone Salka.

TERRY: Careful what you say on the telephone or to anyone in the apartment. That's why I wanted us to talk here. One of those FBI guys began throwing what I said and did in my face.

ERNST: They learned much from the Nazis.

TERRY: Ernst, do you remember back in Paris. With the Nazis on the way. You gave me advice.

ERNST: I told you to get out of the country.

TERRY: I should've listened. Now I'll give you the same advice.

ERNST: This time, will you come with me?

TERRY: I wish I could, but I can't.

ERNST: Please tell me why.

TERRY: From what I hear, once the FBI questions someone, getting out is almost impossible. Get out while you can.

END OF SCENE 4

Scene 5

Scene: *Salka enters Mayer's Office. He is seated at this desk. The book shelves are empty. The desk has nothing on it except a telephone. A 1951 calendar now hangs on the wall. Salka sits in the chair along side the desk.*

MAYER: I'm outta here. You too.

SALKA: Out of here?

MAYER: MGM ain't my show any more. They're kickin' me out. And you.

SALKA: The studio has your name on it.

MAYER: Yeah, yeah. It has Sam Goldwyn's name on it too. You don't see him around here any more, do yah?

SALKA: Who's doing the kicking?

MAYER: The money men. In New York.

SALK: But you made loads of money for those people.

MAYER: I did everything they wanted me to do. It ain't fair.

SALKA: You got rid of talented people who came over here. That wasn't fair.

MAYER: Some of 'em quit.

SALKA: Like they had a choice.

MAYER: All of 'em are a bunch of Commies.

SALKA: For a minute just imagine you are a Jew in Germany. Here's your choice Nazi or Commie. Pick.

MAYER: These days, they shoulda picked the Nazis.

SALKA: I thought I was the writer with the vivid imagination.

MAYER: You had the brains not to join up. They should've too.

SALKA: Looks like staying clear of the Communist menace hasn't done me a whole lot of good.

MAYER: They don't like your friends who weren't so smart. That means they don't like you.

SALKA: The money men in New York don't know I exist.

MAYER: Them Hearst reporters do. They check all the movie credits.

SALKA: For Communists.

MAYER: And "fellow Commie travelers".

SALKA: Whose names they publish.

MAYER: Now yah know how the world works.

SALKA: You could just keep going on your own. Sam Goldwyn did.

MAYER: And lemme guess. You wanna come along.

[*Salka smiles. Mayer shakes his head, no.*]

MAYER: Still gotta keep the money men happy.

SALKA: You could produce for television. The money's there already.

MAYER: I know you think I don't got no standards. With tv, I got 'em.

SALKA: And I'm dying to hear them.

MAYER: *Gone with the Wind*. In black and white. On a screen big as an oversized telephone dial. Who'd watch?

SALKA: More and more people do.

MAYER: All television is good for is black and white movies and a few old vaudeville comics. If you wanna write for that, go ahead. I ain't producin' nothin' for it.

END OF SCENE 5

Scene 6

Scene: *Salka talks on the telephone with Berthold. They are both in hotel rooms, but Salka's looks a good deal more run down than Berthold's. Except for the expensive blue scarf, the same is true of her clothes. Her hair is now gray. Berthold dyes his hair a shiny black. He wears an elegant silk dressing gown. A cane leans on the wall nearby. He has a collection of pill bottles on a night table.*

SALKA: My dearest Berthold. You are so kind to send me money all the way from Vienna.

BERTHOLD: Dearest heart. I adore standing our little world on its head.

SALKA: All I can say is thank you, my darling. Thank you.

BERTHOLD: Please don't take what I say next the wrong way. But, dear heart, there are limits to what I can do.

SALKA: I didn't think you'd found Aladdin's lamp.

BERTHOLD: All those you helped. Surely they can help you for a change.

SALKA: Most can't.

BERTHOLD: What of that composer? I can't remember his name.

SALKA: You mean Ernst?

BERTHOLD: Yes, he's the one. You told me Robbins used his music. Then others did. In the end he must have done very well for himself.

SALKA: Not in the end.

BERTHOLD: What became of him?

SALKA: When you're in Berlin, look him up. The Red hunters drove him out.

BERTHOLD: Did he join Brecht and his Communist friends in east Berlin?

SALKA: He's in west Berlin. The east is too risky. Stalin might get wind of him.

BERTHOLD: Surely there are others who can help.

SALKA: I want to join you.

BERTHOLD: No need to leave your beloved America. No need.

SALKA: We've been apart for so long.

BERTHOLD: I am the modern day version of the wandering Jew, dear heart. You won't see much of me.

SALKA:

> (*Gives a laugh.*)

So much travel. Someone would think you're a courier or a secret agent.

> (*Pause*)

Even though I know you aren't well.

BERTHOLD:

> (*Tries to sound indignant, but ends up giving a suppressed cough.*)

Who says I'm not well?

SALKA: Berthold, I can hear. It must be difficult, my love.

BERTHOLD: Dearest heart, I do what I must to earn a living. Like Arthur Miller's salesman.

> (*Berthold's reference to Death of a Salesman makes Salka gasp. She fights to control the tone of her voice.*)

SALKA: Somewhat belatedly, I shall become your hausfrau. And your nurse. Make you well. Bake your favorite chocolate cake. How can you say no to that?

BERTHOLD: I never could get enough of your chocolate cake. But no. I must say no. Goodbye, dear heart. Goodbye.

> (*Salka hangs up and shakes her head as the lights fade on her. Berthold hangs up the phone, breaks out in a coughing fit and grabs for one of the pill bottles. Lights fade on him.*)

END OF SCENE 6

Scene 7

Scene: *Salka sits in a State Department Office in an uncomfortable chair. She wears conservative looking clothing and no blue scarf. The clothes are old, but presentable.*

Across a massive desk, she faces a sour looking young man sitting in a chair that dwarfs him. He looks rather like a Nazi SS officer in civilian clothes. He dresses in the standard business attire of the 1950s with a white shirt, narrow black tie and a double-breasted, navy blue suit jacket with faint white stripes and wide lapels. The right lapel has an American flag pin through the buttonhole.

Accordion style folders are stacked neatly on his desk. An oversized telephone and a recording device also sit on the desk.

The man looks through papers from a folder.

MAN:

> (*Without looking up.*)

I really don't see how I can help you.

SALKA: I've waited nearly a year for this appointment. I hope you'll at least have the courtesy to hear me out.

MAN:

> (*With obvious reluctance, he picks up the large folder on top, puts it in front of him and thumbs through its papers.*)

Are you still giving the same reason for a passport?

SALKA: I don't understand why your office wants a specific reason. It isn't on the passport request form.

MAN: And I'm asking you if it remains the same.

SALKA: Yes.

MAN: The reason you gave is why we won't grant your passport.

SALKA; Let me be sure I'm understanding you properly. Going to the man I've spent most of my life with. Who's now seriously ill. That's why you're refusing?

MAN: Unfortunately for you, his health counts against you.

SALKA: That makes no sense. It is heartless and cruel.

MAN: I don't believe it's cruel to prevent you from meeting with a Soviet spy who is at his last gasp. And preventing you from acting as his courier.

> (*At first, Salka starts to raise her hand. She obviously wants to shake a finger or even her fist at the man across from her. On second thought, her hand goes back down and she takes a breath.*)

SALKA: Berthold has been many things. But a spy wasn't now one of them. It still isn't.

MAN: I'm afraid we have evidence to the contrary. And as it happens, you provided it.

SALKA: I very much doubt that.

> (*After taking an envelope out of the file on his desk, the State Department man pulls out a small reel of recording tape. He puts it on the machine on his desk. With the volume turned down so that only he can hear it, he listens to the tape for a short time. He stops it, rewinds, stops it again, then turns the volume up and plays so that Salka and the audience can hear her voice.*)

SALKA:

> (*On tape.*)

You are a secret agent.

MAN: Surely you can't deny that is your voice and that's what you said to your husband.

SALKA: To make your case, Berthold needs to say that to me.

MAN: Our anonymous informants have seen your husband consorting with known Communists. In Berlin.

SALKA:

(*Sounding incredulous and amused.*)

Are you talking about Brecht? You can't be serious. He would be the world's worst spy. He can't stay out of the limelight or keep his mouth shut.

MAN: No. Brecht isn't a Jew.

SALKA: What difference does that make?

MAN: It's been our experience that Jews only look out for each other.

SALKA: You obviously haven't encountered Jerry Robbins.

MAN: What are you talking about?

SALKA: Never mind. So who?

MAN: That composer. As soon as he could, he made a beeline for Berlin. And his Soviet employers.

SALKA: You mean Ernst? You think he works for Stalin.

(*Tries unsuccessfully to suppress a laugh.*)

You obviously have no idea how utterly tone deaf you are.

MAN: Let me play you something else.

(*The voice of Ernst come from the recorder.*)

ERNST: I'm still a Communist.

MAN: That doesn't sound like a man who hates the Soviets. Then, of course, we know your sentiments as well.

(*He again switches on the tape recorder, listens, then turns up the volume.*)

SALKA: I belonged to one of those groups. The Communist ran it. Stalin and the Soviets are our friends.

(*State Department man stops tape.*)

SALKA: I would like to know what you think my political views are.

MAN: Before we actually went to war, you were a premature antifascist.

SALKA: You almost make it sound like a sexual perversion.

MAN: The devil may have many faces, Mrs. Viertel, but he's still the devil. And it's not like you're naive or innocent about such matters.

SALKA: My politics. Or Berthold's. They shouldn't have anything to do with issuing me a passport.

MAN: Whether or not you and your husband are loyal to this country matters to us more than any thing else.

SALKA: Evidently it's hopeless to expect caring for a dying man to play any part.

MAN: Probably because of your husband's poor health, he hasn't transmited any of the information. We will not help you get it.

SALKA: You actually believe Berthold will give me this imaginary information. And what? I'll give it to Greta Garbo.

MAN:

(*Grabs a pen and a note pad and furiously scribbles a short note.*)

Who's she?

SALKA:

(*Shakes her head and sighs.*)

The irony of what is going on here doesn't escape me.

MAN: What irony?

SALKA: Since you were in diapers, the United States government has done everything it can not to let Jews in. Now you won't let me out.

MAN: I will tell you honestly, if we could, we would lock you up as a spy.

SALKA: One more try. If I was a spy, do you really think that I'd travel under my own name?

MAN: If you're threatening to get a false passport. I hope you do. Then we'll finally put you in prison.

SALKA: I can get a genuine passport.

MAN: I certainly won't issue you one.

SALKA: Perhaps it's slipped by you. As a Jew, I can go to the Israeli embassy, claim citizenship in Israel and, quite legally, use their passport. When I do, I'm sure many reporters would want to know why.

> (*The State Department man looks stunned and says nothing as the lights fade.*)

END OF SCENE 6

Scene 7

Scene: *Setting and costumes are identical to the first scene in the first act.*

SALKA: I still find it hard. You, a Jew, back to Berlin. After all that's happened.

> (*Ernst starts to say something but Salka raises her hand to stop him.*)

And before you say anything. Yes. I know you always considered yourself German first and Jewish last. But the Germans didn't.

> (*Pause*)

And don't?

ERNST: You know Berlin never really accepted Hitler and the Nazis the way the rest of Germany did. Our mayor now, Willi Brandt. A fellow anti-Nazi exile. They elected him anyway.

SALKA: I'll bet when you came back, they didn't elect you to anything. Or throw you a party.

ERNST: In Berlin they let me live in peace. So maybe it isn't so bad that I had to leave your favorite country.

SALKA: I'll never forgive those bastards for what they did to you and the others.

ERNST: Like so many other countries, America threw me out. I rather came to expect it.

SALKA: You say the Germans in Berlin let you live in peace. Is that your polite way of saying everyone pretends you're not there?

ERNST: The people around me now have no idea who I am. They let me get on with my life.

SALKA: Sounds to me like you've become an exile in your home country.

ERNST: I admit, if Terry could have come back with me, it would have been better.

SALKA: If the Red Scare ever vanishes, then the government will let him join you.

ERNST: That government did everything they could to make living in the U.S. impossible for you.

SALKA: They did.

ERNST: And then they caused you unnamed difficulties getting here.

SALKA: It's a sad story. But if you want to know...

ERNST:

(*Cutting in quickly.*)

Yes, I do.

SALKA: The Israelis seemed like the only option I had to leave. But in the end, I couldn't bring myself to go to them.

ERNST: It must have been hard for you. Not going to Berthold.

SALKA: I couldn't do it. I just couldn't.

ERNST: You know I never considered Israel as a refuge.

SALKA: Because you never felt Jewish enough?

ERNST: Because as a man who feels like a German, I had no desire to put myself at the mercy of that pack of vicious East European Jews who run the place.

SALKA: It's honest of you to say so. But a little terrifying.

ERNST: Maybe that's my roundabout way of saying I don't want to start over yet once again.

SALKA: I can understand that.

ERNST: Unlike you, I don't have the stamina.

SALKA: I would give a great deal not to need it.

ERNST: But here you are. With your instincts as a screen writer still intact.

SALKA: Why do you say that?

ERNST: You have built up the suspense. Will you please tell me how you got to this side of the Atlantic.

SALKA: Believe it or not, the State Department people had this fantasy. That Berthold spied for the Soviets. And I was his would-be courier.

(*Ernst gives a short laugh and shakes his head.*)

SALKA: When Berthold died, their excuse for withholding my U.S. passport vanished.

ERNST: You helped so many people. Now it is our turn to help you go back and live.

SALKA: You are all so talented. You did well. My reward is I helped.

ERNST: That is my point. Some of us did succeed.

SALKA: You have your own worries. Like poor Stephan Zweig and his wife. You remember them, don't you?

ERNST: Of course.

SALKA: Then you know. Successful. But after years in exile, both of them committed suicide. None of you need my worries too.

ERNST: If you had felt that way, we would be ashes in some concentration camp.

SALKA: All you lovely people I helped so many, many years ago. Lost contact with one another. I'm sure.

ERNST: It is you who matters.

SALKA: After all this time, I wouldn't feel right begging for help.

ERNST: So many good deeds. You were, indeed, punished for them.

SALKA: You know, that saying about good deeds and punishment. It's wrong.

ERNST: If I was in your position, I don't know if I would say that.

SALKA: No, no. I'm not being punished for the good deeds.

ERNST: So how would you describe what has happened to you?

SALKA: Jews and exile. Over many, many years, we've come to know each other very, very well. I've renewed our acquaintance.

END OF PLAY

MARGERY MEETS HARRY

CHARACTERS:

Margery
Fred
Earl
Mrs. Crandon
Dr. Leroy Crandon
Evelyn Richardson
Mark Richardson
Harry Houdini
Hereward Carrington

Scene 1

Scene: *MARGERY puts a great deal of effort into washing a sheet in a large tub. The sleeves of her cheap dress are rolled up to her shoulders and she's all wet. The room is filled with clothes drying on a series of clothes lines strung through the room. When she finishes washing, also with great effort, she wrings the excess water out of the sheet and throws it across a vacant space on a clothes line. Margery then looks at an expensive dress hanging nearby, takes it from the clothes line, presses it against her body and dances about. Enter her brother, FRED. His face is bruised, a bit of blood runs out of the corner of his mouth.*

FRED: Little sister Margery, little sister Margery you're gonna get in a whole lot of trouble if daddy walks in and finds you playin' with Mrs. Prescott's best dress.

> [*After a couple of more spins with the dress, Margery stops and notices her brother's injuries. She starts to walk toward him, but he puts his hand up to stop her.*]

MARGERY: He do that to you?

FRED: Yeah. Who else?

MARGERY: Do I have to tell again? Don't let 'im get you in a corner

> [*Margery hangs up the dress and again begins struggling with the sheet.*]

FRED: I ain't as quick as you.

MARGERY: So are you just goin' to go on lettin' him beat on you?

FRED: I'm goin' to take off.

MARGERY: If daddy catches you...

FRED: He won't. I ain't quick, but I'm sneaky.

MARGERY: So then he takes it out on me. Thanks.

FRED: First he's got to catch you.

MARGERY: If you can figure a way to hang around, you'll get the farm.

FRED: Farmin' a farm that has more rocks than dirt. And drinkin' away my sorrows like him. No thanks. Even if he dropped dead tomorrow and left this place to both of us, what we gonna do with it?

MARGERY: Farm the rocks. Get married. Have kids. Make 'em wash other people's stuff to make ends meet.

> [*Margery stops struggling with the sheet and turns to face Fred.*]

FRED: So I'm leavin'.

MARGERY: For where? He ain't just goin' to let you go.

FRED: He'll never find me.

MARGERY: How d' you know that?

FRED: Because I signed up as a stage hand with the vaudeville show that's passin' through town.

> [*Margery takes the remainder of the wet laundry out of the tub and throws it on the floor. Fred looks surprised.*]

MARGERY: Take me with you.

FRED: What?

MARGERY: You heard me. Take me with you.

FRED: You plannin' on being a stage hand too? I don't think they'll let girls be stage hands.

MARGERY: They got girls doin' other things, don't they?

FRED: Sure, but I never heard you sing on key or dance like a showgirl or tell jokes anyone thought was funny.

MARGERY: No. But that's not all they got for me to do. They got jugglers and dogs jumpin' through hoops. They got magicians. Don't they?

FRED: Come on little sister. Are you tellin' me you can do any of that?

MARGERY: 'course not. But somebody's got to take care of the juggler's equipment, look after the dogs. And the magician's got to saw some girl in half, don't he?

FRED: You really think you can talk your way into some job?

MARGERY: Take me with you and we'll find out.

FRED: If they take you on, you know and I know it won't really be because they want you to feed the dogs. They'll have somethin' else in mind for a pretty thing like you.

MARGERY: Yeah, I figured that out too.

FRED: And I'm supposed to just sit there and let them do it?

MARGERY: You think I'm just gonna lay back and let 'em?

FRED: You think they'll give you a choice?

MARGERY: Big brother, I'm the one who's got the choice.

END OF SCENE 1

Scene 2

Scene: *Kitchen of Margery's apartment in Boston, years later. The kitchen is basic, no frills. The sink has a pump, not a faucet. The curtains on the window over the sink have seen better days. Margery and Fred are seated at kitchen table, arm wrestling.*

FRED: Give up little sister.

MARGERY: That's the only way you'll win.

FRED: You wish.

> [*At the sound of telephone ringing, Fred relaxes his arm and Margery slams his hand to the table.*]

Wait a minute. You don't have a phone. How did you...?

MARGERY: When the magician wasn't sawin' me in half, I picked up a few things.

FRED: All right, I'll have t' do it.

MARGERY: What?

FRED: Call in the spirits.

MARGERY: The spirits?

FRED: Yeah, the spirits. Now hold both my hands and close your eyes.

> [*Margery follows Fred instructions and when she does, the kitchen table jumps into the air and crashes down.*]

MARGERY: How did you...?

FRED: I didn't do anything little sister.

MARGERY: Like I didn't make the phone ring?

FRED: Don't you wish we could've stuck with vaudeville? It was so much fun.

MARGERY: Yeah, too bad the money ain't dependable. The men ain't either.

FRED: Would I ever say, "I told you so?"

MARGERY: Not and live to say it again.

FRED: You aren't suffering under the delusion that the men outside vaudeville are any different?

MARGERY: Depends on the man, doesn't it?

FRED: You think your grocery man, fits the bill better? What's his name?

MARGERY:

> [*Shifts to a less provincial accent.*]

Earl. Margery and Earl. Sounds like we fit together, doesn't it?

FRED: You're gonna to have to do more than sound hoity-doity to fit into his world.

MARGERY: I know.

FRED: You gonna teach him he can do more things on his knees with you besides pray?

MARGERY: Now don't keep makin' fun of him, Freddy. Earl's a very nice man. Respectable, something you and me ain't never goin' to be on our own.

FRED: Respectable. Nice 'n dull.

MARGERY: Well, that's why I keep you around big brother. For entertainment.

FRED: How you gonna keep your respectable husband entertained? Show him you can do the splits or kick a gentleman's hat off his head?

MARGERY: As far as Earl knows, I'm a farm girl who came to the big city and got a job the library. That's where he found me. And let's keep it that way big brother.

FRED: He won't hear about your wicked past in vaudeville from me.

[*Margery blows Fred a kiss.*]

FRED: So you really goin' to marry him?

MARGERY: He's the best that's come along.

FRED: So far.

MARGERY: He's a definite step up from magicians and ventriloquists. I didn't come here to Boston to wait around for the perfect man and end up dying in a place like this.

FRED: You need a guy just like me to spice up your life.

MARGERY: Freddy, you're one of a kind.

FRED: So marry me.

MARGERY: You'd better get to the railyard and stop foolin' around or they'll dock your pay again for bein' late.

[*Fred reluctantly gets up, goes over to Margery and kisses her on the forehead.*]

FRED: I gotta tell yah. With all those steam engines chugging around the yard, tryin' to get the right freight cars hitched to the right engine, it ain't vaudeville, but it keeps me on my toes. If I zig instead of zag, all I'll be is a spirit.

MARGERY: Well, you could always get your friends who are already spirits to drop those cars down in the right place.

[*Exit Fred*]

END OF SCENE 2

Scene 3

Scene: *Earl's Shop. Margery and EARL enter and then stand center stage. They wear serviceable, but not particularly stylish overcoats. Earl has a moustache that curls up at the ends and wears a derby hat. On one side is the meat section where dead animals of various descriptions hang from hooks behind a large butcher bloc. Meat cutting instruments lie on the block. On the other side of the store are shelved grocery items. Earl gestures expansively as he begins to speak.*

EARL: Here it is. Just look around.

MARGERY: If you're as proud as you look, only a magician could keep the buttons from popping right off your coat.

EARL: Well, I am proud. Why shouldn't I be?

MARGERY: Sorry. Just having a little fun.

EARL: I know, I know, sweety. It's just that next to you, this place is the most important thing in my life. [*Embarrassed pause*] Sorry, sorry. I didn't mean you're a thing. What I'm trying to say...

MARGERY: It's all right. I know. I know.

[*Gives Earl a hug and a kiss on the cheek.*]

EARL: You remember. I told you. I started out with a push cart and now I've got all this place. And I'm not done growing. Oh, the plans I have! Would you believe...

MARGERY: You know I believe in you.

EARL: And you'll help me get where I want to go?

MARGERY: Tell me where that is. Don't hold back. In your wildest dreams, tell me what you see.

EARL: I want this store to become the place where all the people really matter in Boston go for their food. I want to be able to sit in an office where I can plan to make things even better because I've a first-class staff who make the customers feel so good that they'll keep coming back.

MARGERY: Sounds really swell.

EARL: And you'll really help?

MARGERY: Of course.

EARL: Oh, thank you, thank you, thank you. Because to start out I can't afford to hire all those staff and I can't do everything myself. I really need your help here.

MARGERY: You mean like running the cash register, that sort of thing?

EARL: To start with, I thought I'd do that. I had something else in mind for you.

MARGERY: What?

> [*Lights go down and then come up. Margery stands behind a large butcher block with the large leg of beef on it. She wears a blood smeared apron and the long selves of her dress are rolled up to her shoulders. Using a meat cleaver, with just one whack, she cuts saleable pieces of meat from the leg. After she cuts off half a dozen of pieces, Earl enters.*]

EARL: Is that for Doctor Crandon and his wife?

MARGERY: Well, not all of it. There's a war on.

EARL:

> [*Earl looks stunned by the remark. When he recovers, he rushes his reply.*]

I tried to go, Margery. You know I tried to go. But they wouldn't take me.

MARGERY: Whoa, whoa, Earl. It's okay. Honest. I know you tried.

EARL: If I just had all my own teeth, they would've takin' me.

MARGERY: I know. It's okay.

EARL: I try real hard to look on the bright side of what's going on.

MARGERY: The bright side of a war?

EARL: Oh, you know what I mean. We all had to learn new things. Like you learned to drive the delivery van. You've said you even like it.

MARGERY: Look, why don't I wrap up a couple of chops for the Crandons and you can deliver them and the rest of the Back Bay orders.

EARL: You sure that's okay with you? I know how much you like drivin' the delivery van.

MARGERY: As they keep telling us. War is a time of sacrifice. You go. Butter up the Crandons. Everybody looks up to them.

EARL: Good idea. If I get on the good side of him, he could really throw some important people my way.

END OF SCENE 3

Scene 4

Scene: *Kitchen of the Crandon house. Earl stands in a elaborate kitchen. The meat he brought sits on a table. MRS. CRANDON enters. A woman in her early thirties, her dress is a bit too elegant for sitting about the house. She carries a half-full high-ball glass.*

MRS. CRANDON: My maid said you refused to leave unless I came to speak with you.

EARL: I'm sorry. I didn't mean to sound rude. It's just that I wanted to thank you personally for your patronage.

MRS. CRANDON: The cook maid buys the food. For some reason my husband has insisted on selecting the meat personally. Any way, that's his story to me.

EARL: I see him in my place about once a week.

MRS. CRANDON: It seems to me he takes his time, presumably at your establishment.

EARL: He's really selective. I just kind of presumed that you told him what you wanted.

MRS. CRANDON: The would-be famous Dr. Crandon hasn't done what I wanted for a long time.

[*Shakes here head.*]

If he didn't make up his tales about the butcher shop, it'll be an all time first.

EARL: I'm always glad to bring my customers good news.

MRS. CRANDON:

[*More to herself than to Earl*]

I still have friends at the hospital from when I was a nurse. I have them call me, let me know when he's on his way home. Thought he was up to something on Mondays 'cause it took him too long to get home. Probably is.

[*Now to Earl*]

MRS. CRANDON: Ever hired a private detective? Know where I could find a good one?

EARL:

> [*Begins to feel uncomfortable. Looks for a way to exit at least semi-gracefully.*]

Like I said, sorry to bother you. Maybe I should thank Dr. Crandon, ask him to pass the word along about my shop.

MRS. CRANDON: Yeah, why don't you do that. Pass along my regards too.

END OF SCENE 4

Scene 5

Scene: *Earl's store. Margery wraps up a couple of pieces of meat and goes back to chopping. When CRANDON enters, she stops.*

CRANDON: Hello, Margery.

MARGERY: Dr. Crandon. I've got to apologize. I just sent Earl off with your order. I must've forgotten you were stopping by for it.

CRANDON: No need to apologize. My rather confused wife doesn't always remember to pass along messages. I knew I'd finish up early at the hospital, so I thought I'd drop by in person.

MARGERY: Now, if you'd walked through that door two minutes earlier, you and Earl would've run smack into each other and your dinner would've ended up on the floor. So I guess it's a good thing you got here when you did.

CRANDON: You've quite an imagination, Margery.

MARGERY: Must be a family trait. My brother Fred had lots, until he got between a locomotive and a freight car.

CRANDON: Sorry to hear that.

MARGERY: I guess he was too much of a dreamer for his own good.

CRANDON: We all have dreams Margery. I'm sure you have them too.

MARGERY: Most of mine are kind of private, but, if you promise you won't laugh, I've got one you might get a kick out of hearing one.

> [*Crandon smiles, then pretends to wipe the smile off his face and ends up looking theatrically serious.*]

MARGERY: My dream is to drive one of those new fangled tanks in General Pershing's army and win the war single-handed.

CRANDON: Then I suppose there's the victory parade that goes around the Common with you leading it.

MARGERY: Yeah, that's a nice touch. I'll try not to have the dream while I'm drivin' the delivery van.

CRANDON: If you're willing to take your dream down a notch or two, I just might be able to make it come true.

MARGERY: I didn't think serious doctors like you were into kiddin'.

CRANDON: No. Really. When the hospital ships come back from France, they've got hundreds and hundreds of wounded soldiers on them. We need ambulance drivers to take them to the hospitals.

MARGERY: Putting somethin' alive back together instead of choppin' up dead meat. That sounds good to me.

> [*Margery takes a whack at the animal leg in front of her and cuts off another piece of meat.*]

Make for a nice change.

CRANDON: Of course I often go on these ambulance runs. It would mean seeing a lot more of me.

MARGERY: I think I could live with that.

CRANDON: The hospital ships don't always get in on time. You could find yourself waiting with me in the ambulance for a long time with nothing to do.

MARGERY: Really?

CRANDON: Really. The question is, what will we do to pass the time.

MARGERY: Between your brains and my imagination, I'm sure we'll think of something.

CRANDON: What about your husband?

MARGERY: Earl? What about him?

CRANDON: Can he spare you? You seem to do a lot around here.

MARGERY: More than I planned.

CRANDON: Maybe it would be better if I asked him. I could tell him it would help the war effort and all that. Tell him I can find a way to see to it he gets paid to hire temporary help.

MARGERY: Actually, if he thought you owed him a favor, I expect he'd find a way.

END OF SCENE 5

Scene 6

Scene: *Back of an ambulance. Boston harbor is visible through the front window. Margery gets dressed while Crandon puts on his white doctor's coat over his clothes and then combs his hair. He holds up a hand mirror and smiles.*

MARGERY: I take it you've noticed that I've never asked if you loved me.

CRANDON: Honestly, until now, I hadn't thought about it. Now that I am thinking about it, I do find it a bit insulting that you never even asked. Are you trying to pick a fight?

MARGERY: No. The ship's still a long ways out and we'd be stuck here fuming at each other until it arrived. But do you want to know why I never brought it up?

CRANDON: Now that you ask.

MARGERY: Because then you'd presume that I loved you and of course I don't.

CRANDON: I thought you just said you weren't trying to pick a fight. So then why are you bringing all this up?

MARGERY: Just looking ahead to the end of the war and ambulance rides. To when both of us can say it's been fun in the sack. And fooling our so-called better halves.

CRANDON: And both wife number one and number two called me cold blooded.

MARGERY: Look, both of us came into this for some fun, with our eyes wide open. Didn't we?

CRANDON: Well I did.

MARGERY: And tell me honestly, weren't you thinking something along the lines of beginning a little speech to me with, "It's been fun." I'm sure a man of your experience has a standard speech you give the girls at the end.

> [*Margery finishes dressing, picks up the mirror Crandon used and applies make-up, then straightens her hair.*]

CRANDON: But what if I don't see things coming to an end?

MARGERY: Come on, Really?

CRANDON: Why end the fun?

MARGERY: What? In some hotel room. With both of us watching the clock? That wouldn't be nearly as much fun as entertaining each other in the back of an ambulance until some ship that's always late finally docks.

CRANDON: No, I had something different in mind.

MARGERY: Like?

CRANDON: Divorce our current spouses.

MARGERY: There's that sneaky sense of humor of yours.

CRANDON: I'm quite serious.

MARGERY: So what happens when we get bored with each other in bed? And we will. You know we will.

CRANDON: We'll be like Louis XV and Madame Pompadour. Friends and allies against the rest of the world.

MARGERY: You know, of course, that I don't have any idea what you're talking about.

CRANDON: It doesn't matter. You and I are so much alike, it scares me. We may not love each other, but we fascinate each other. Always wondering what the other one will do next.

MARGERY: Okay. Let's get practical. A respectable man like you. The people in your set might wink at a mistress. But a divorce? You'll drive your patients away. Harvard would throw you out.

CRANDON: I've divorced before. Do I look like I'm begging on some street corner?

MARGERY: But I bet your family disowned you.

CRANDON: Are you really saying that you're worried about your family? Take my word for it, having a daughter marry a wealthy doctor-professor will go a long way toward helping them get over the so-called scandal.

MARGERY: My brother, Fred's, the only member of my family I ever cared about and he's dead.

CRANDON: And then there's your husband.

MARGERY: Yes, and then there's Earl.

CRANDON: Do you love him? If you do, you hide it well.

MARGERY: I could go on living with him.

CRANDON: I'll take that as a no. But does he love you?

MARGERY: In the beginning, I guess he did. Now the only thing he loves is his market. I'm supposed to help him make it the most successful one in Boston. I don't think he'll take my leaving very well.

CRANDON: Well then, how about this? After my divorce is final, I'll find a way to convince him to let you go.

MARGERY: He is a butcher and he won't be happy. Do you plan to go armed?

CRANDON: He's a loser who knows he's a loser. I'll tell him I can make it worth his while and he'll feel like a winner. I think he'll find finally becoming a winner hard to resist.

MARGERY: I take it you think that money buys everything.

CRANDON: Do I believe everyone has a price they will find irresistible? Yes, yes I do. But do you know what beats money almost every time?

MARGERY: Not much in my world.

CRANDON: Status. Where those who matter in your little world see you on the big world's totem pole.

MARGERY: Is that what you think you're doing with me? Offering me a price I'll find irresistible? You think letting you shape how the world looks at me 'll do it?

CRANDON: You've already come a long way from that little farm you've told me about. I do believe you're curious to find out just how far you can go.

MARGERY: Some how or other, things have gone from mutual fascination to my ambitions.

CRANDON: Unless I've misjudged you, you like a challenge. And here's yours. See how long you can keep me fascinated.

MARGERY: A man who's looking to take on his third wife seems unlikely to change his ways.

CRANDON: Nor is a woman who views men as play toys.

MARGERY: So what's supposed to hold us together.

CRANDON: The adventure of finding something outside the bedroom that fascinates us both.

MARGERY: I'll admit it. Now you've aroused my curiosity.

CRANDON: You won't regret it. I promise you, you won't regret it. I'd be very surprised if Margery the curious cat has come anywhere near exhausting her nine lives.

END OF SCENE 6

Scene 7

Scene: *The library of the Crandon home in Back BayBoston. Crandon and MARK RICHARDSON are in the library at a large oak desk. Crandon, seated, looks at a book with Mark looking over Crandon's. Margery and EVELYN RICHARDSON enter, each carrying many packages. Both women are dressed in elegant 1920s style. Margery wears a dress that looks very much like the one with which she danced in Scene 1. The two women fling themselves into well padded arm chairs and drop their packages to the floor.*

CRANDON: Well my dear, I see that unlike the German mark, the 1923 American dollar has lost none of its value.

> [*Crandon gets up from the desk, goes to Margery, bends down and kisses her on the lips. She then puts her hand in back of his head and returns the kiss. Crandon then goes back to his desk chair.*]

MARGERY: Now, now. Money aside, isn't part of your fascination trying to figure out what I'll look like next?

CRANDON: The eternal shape shifter. A kind of ethereal presence who drifts into a room then floats out.

EVELYN: Doctor-Professor Crandon, you sound more like a someone taking part in a seance than a man of science.

MARK: Funny thing you should mention it, but...

EVELYN: Don't tell me you two were holding a seance while we were gone.

CRANDON: Actually, your husband and I have been discussing an area that most pure scientists would never admit even exists.

EVELYN: All right, you've created the suspense. If I had a drum and cymbals, I would give them a solid bang as a prelude. This area is?

MARK: Spiritualism, darling, spiritualism.

EVELYN: That hardly seems your style, either of you.

MARK: Not mine, any way.

CRANDON: Let's say I'm arguing for an open mind.

MARGERY: My, my. Any particular spirit interest you? Louis XV maybe?

CRANDON: Not a single person. It's the whole idea of the spirits of the dead inhabiting a world parallel to ours.

MARGERY: Now if I were the professor and you were the student...

CRANDON: We've played that game, haven't we?

MARGERY: We usually play doctor and nurse. But as I was saying, if I was the professor, I'd want my student to give me proof.

MARK: Ah, there's the rub. I made the same point. Without some definitive proof, it's all mere speculation.

CRANDON: Carnival quacks aside, I think there must be a way to communicate with this parallel world.

MARGERY: If it exists.

EVELYN: And on that happy note, we must be off. The cook threatened to quit if we let her dinner go cold one more time.

MARK: Yes, yes. He who fights and runs away, lives to fight another day. Cheerio sparing partner, and Margery too.

[*Exit Evelyn and Mark*]

MARGERY: You never cease to surprise me.

CRANDON: You mean my interest in spiritualism, my dear? What's so surprising?

MARGERY: You spend your days looking at the tiniest bits of the real world through a microscope and now you want to find something that's probably not there? I'll stick with surprising.

CRANDON: We now know that the world is made up of atoms. They are so small even our most powerful microscopes can't see them. Yet we know they are there. What if when we die, our bodily atoms fall away, but our spiritual atoms remain connected together?

MARGERY: Let's say you're right. Let's say there's a spirit world we can't see. How will we ever know?

CRANDON: Some how or other, we'll communicate with them and equally as important, they'll communicate with us. There's your challenge. Find a way for me to talk with the spirits of the dead.

MARGERY: Next you're going to want me to invent a bomb that's so big and terrible that there'll never be another world war.

CRANDON: You leave the atoms to me. Why don't you see if you can figure out a way to communicate with the spirits. Talking with people is your strong suit. Talk to the spirits.

MARGERY: I can talk all I want. The trick is to get them to talk back. This isn't a joke? You really want to do this?

CRANDON: I'll be honest with you. The things of this world increasingly bore me.

MARGERY: Says the man of science.

CRANDON: Says the man of science. I feel like I'm doing the same things over and over again and only inching forward. Few care. No one notices.

MARGERY: And you want me to find something that will keep the Crandons in the limelight with a great leap forward. All I have to do is make the dead speak to us.

CRANDON: It's a fascination we can both share. But right now I'm not waiting around for spiritual conversation. I'm off to the hospital.

[*Crandon gets up from his chair and walks toward the library door.*]

MARGERY: Surgery? At dinner hour?

CRANDON: A private consultation.

MARGERY: Well, I know how these private consultations, so often with young women, can tire you out.

[*A slight smile creeps onto Crandon's face.*]

Don't come home too exhausted. You never know what the evening might bring.

CRANDON: My dear, I promise. I shall be very quick.

[*Crandon kisses Margery on the forehead and exits. After he leaves, Margery goes over to his desk, sits down in his chair, picks up a book on spiritualism that lies there and begins reading as the lights fade.*]

END OF SCENE 7

Scene 8

Scene: *Dining room of the Crandon house. Margery, Crandon, Evelyn and Mark are seated around a dining room table with after dinner drinks in their hands.*

MARK: So, had any more thoughts on how to make contact with the spirits of the dead? Something new and revolutionary?

CRANDON: I have wondered if they'd respond to radio waves.

MARK: You mean create one of those new fangled radio stations and rig it to just broadcast to the spirits? Of course they'd need to have their own radios and radio stations so that they could broadcast back to us.

EVELYN: I know all this is supposed to be beyond a simple woman, but do you have any idea how silly spirit radio stations sound?

MARGERY: I've been doing a lot of reading. If there is such a thing, nobody has written anything about it.

MARK: Okay, so what have they written about?

MARGERY: Something simple.

MARK: Simple, like what?

MARGERY: The traditional seance. You know. We make the room dark. Then all of us hold hands and each of us ask the spirits to let us know they can hear us.

CRANDON: You mean just like every carnival fraud does?

EVELYN: I read this article about Harry Houdini, you know the magician, escape artist. He thinks there are real mediums. He's trying to find an honest one so he can talk with his late mother.

MARGERY: That's it. What if these self-described mediums are doing the right thing, but because they're fakes, the spirits wouldn't talk to them?

MARK: A former librarian, a housewife and two men of science. No carnival tricksters in this room.

EVELYN: It's worth a try.

CRANDON: All right, all right. In the spirit of pure scientific enquiry, let's see if we can contact the spirits with a seance.

MARGERY: Why don't we put a lit candelabra on the table and then turn off the lights. Let's each pick a person who we wish was still here and take turns trying to make contact. We can hold hands to give each other strength and as a guarantee that none of us are playing tricks.

EVELYN: Sounds exciting. Let's do it.

> [*Crandon fetches a candelabra, puts it on the table and lights it. Then he switches off the electric lights. After he sits down again, all four of them hold hands. The candelabra only lights the lower half of their faces and puts their eyes in deep shadow.*]

MARGERY; Who wants to start?

EVELYN: I will. Eileen? Eileen? If you can hear me now, let me know.

CRANDON: Wait a minute. Who's this Eileen?

EVELYN: Just after the war, my younger sister, Eileen, died of the Spanish flu and I've always missed her terribly. Okay, okay, here it goes again. Eileen, now's the time to let me know you're there.

> [*Pause*]

MARK: I guess not. Margery, go ahead.

MARGERY: Big brother Fred. If you're around, let me know.

CRANDON: I believe the spiritualists say, give me a sign.

MARK: Shush!

MARGERY: Give me a sign.

> [*Pause. Then the table thumps and the flames on the candelabra waver.*]

MARGERY: Fred!

CRANDON: How do we know it's your brother?

EVELYN: Margery, ask him a question only the two of you would know the right answer to.

MARGERY: Fred, did I work for the Salvation Army when I came to Boston? Knock once for yes and twice for no.

> [*The table thumps twice.*]

MARGERY: Did I work as a librarian?

> [*The table thumps once.*]

MARK: That's right!

MARGERY: So what now?

CRANDON: I know what this looks like, but I'm still trying to get my mind around what's happened here.

EVELYN; Ever the skeptical scientist. Looks like? Come on. What more do you want?

CRANDON: All right. Let's say Margery is a medium for her brother's spirit. But where does that get us?

MARK: It gets us in contact with the spirit world. That's what you wanted to happen, isn't it?

CRANDON: But what kind of contact? Table thumping is a rather unsatisfactory way of communicating. How are we to get answers to questions that go beyond yes or no?

MARK: Maybe the spirit of Fred knows Morse code. Margery, why don't you ask.

MARGERY: Fred, do you know Morse code?

[*The table thumps twice.*]

EVELYN: Well, what about having him thump once for an "a" and twice for a "b" and so on up the alphabet?

CRANDON: And then we could sit here half the night while he thumps out that he saw a zebra at the Kalamazoo zoo.

FRED (V.O.): I don't know how to break this to you, Leroy, but the only zoo I ever went to was here in Boston.

END OF SCENE 8

Scene 9

Scene: *Crandon's dining room. Crandon and Margery having an after dinner drink.*

CRANDON: The others will be here in an hour.

MARGERY: Do I know any of them or have we exhausted the supply of Harvard's doctors.

CRANDON: A couple of repeats from last week who seemed particularly amused by your brother's outrageous remarks. But the main attraction tonight, besides yourself of course, will be the people from William James's group.

MARGERY: I don't remember you mentioning that you knew them.

CRANDON: Until the word got out about you, I don't think they would have given me the time of day. But they actually invited me to lunch and we had quite a nice chat.

MARGERY: You do know that ultimately all the people at the university who are curious about me and Fred will have satisfied their curiosity.

CRANDON: What do you think will happen then?

MARGERY: You'll be much less pleased when the Will James set finds other luncheon partners.

CRANDON: Perhaps the fascination will be gone. One day.

MARGERY: One day soon. They'll get bored and move on. And you'll need to do the same.

CRANDON: But, much as it pains me to admit it, there is a world beyond Harvard and in it your fame as the genuine medium has spread.

MARGERY: I take it you've heard the expression, quit while you're ahead. We've played this...

CRANDON: What do you mean "played this?" These seances are strictly on the up and up. You're the medium who never takes money. What fake would do that?

MARGERY: What I mean is that's it's become a game. The people who come here are skeptics. They're looking for a way to figure out the trick. Do you really want to take the voice, that is to say, the spirit of Fred into the big wide world?

CRANDON: But it's there already. At least its reputation is. Just the other day I had letter from Sir Arthur Conan Doyle saying his friends here said all kinds of flattering things about you.

MARGERY: The man who did the Sherlock Holmes stories? What's there here that would interest him?

CRANDON: He lost his son in the war and has been trying to contact him ever since. Like that Houdini fellow, he's always looking for an honest medium.

MARGERY: So, you see us going to England and holding a private seance for Conan Doyle?

CRANDON: I see us going wherever there are scientifically minded people who wish to expand their horizons and who are willing to have earnest conversations about the possibilities.

MARGERY: With you at the center of it all.

CRANDON: It is fascinating to see just how far this will go. And of course you're a major part of the fascination. For me and for the others.

MARGERY: Won't all of this travel with me cut into your private consulting time?

CRANDON: That's the thing about consulting. It's always possible to pick it up again. But there are ways to help insure my fascination will last longer.

MARGERY: Do tell.

CRANDON: The journal, Scientific America, is offering a prize that equals about a years pay for an ordinary mortal. That is, if that ordinary mortal can honestly contact the spirit world. I'm going to ask Sir Arthur to nominate you for the prize.

MARGERY: Since no would ever call you or me ordinary and you have all the money we could ever possibly spend in a lifetime, why bother?

CRANDON: Oh, I'll donate the prize to charity. But the prestige of winning that prize will carry us a long way. The whole world of learning will be there for the taking.

MARGERY: If I win the prize, why do I feel like I will become something like a performing monkey on a worldwide tour?

CRANDON: When you win the contest, you'll become the equivalent of a powerful telescope that enables the world to see things never seen before.

MARGERY: You make winning the contest sound like winning a Nobel Prize.

CRANDON: For me, it will be. All you have to do is convince the prize committee.

MARGERY: And they are?

CRANDON: There are several people on it. But two influential members will undoubtedly sway the rest. A man named Hereward Carrington who's exposed many fake English mediums. And then there's Harry Houdini.

MARGERY: I like this idea even less than starting a traveling circus.

CRANDON: You keep reacting as if this is some kind prank we're playing. It's a scientific break through and I'm...we're the force driving it.

MARGERY: If your scientific friends were curious and amused, they had no real stake in digging very deep. This contest has a couple of judges who literally make their way in the world by uncovering fakes. Has it occurred to you that once they've found an honest medium, they're out of business.

END OF SCENE 9

Scene 10

Scene: *A dark room. The stage is dark. A luminescent green object that looks like a small flying saucer hovers in air then moves back and forth and up and down.*

VOICE: I've arrived to bring you my message from beyond.

> [*A two flashlights go on pointing above the object. Then there is the repeating sound of a pump spray bottle. The flashlights then pick up reflections of water droplets dripping from the very thin wires that support the floating object. The object crashes to a table with a bang. Foots steps run and a door bangs. The lights go on. HARRY HOUDINI and HEREWARD CARRINGTON, flashlights in hand, stand there. Both are smiling.*]

END OF SCENE 10

Scene 11

Scene: *Crandon's dining room. Margery, Crandon, Houdini and Carrington are seated at the dinner table. Crandon holds a brandy decanter and each of the men have a brandy snifters in front of them.*

CRANDON: Carrington?

CARRINGTON: Yes, please.

> [*Crandon fills about a third of the brandy snifter.*]

CRANDON: Houdini?

HOUDINI: Thank you, but I think not.

CRANDON: Your loss. My wine merchant tells me this brandy was Napoleon's favorite.

> [*Crandon pours himself considerably less than he poured Carrington.*]

HOUDINI: I take it your wine merchant has availed himself of your wife's services. But, thank you, I must say no. A sound body and a clear mind. In my profession, it's what keeps me alive. I see Mrs. Crandon is like me.

MARGERY: Oh, yes. I never drink before a seance.

HOUDINI: Seance? I thought the seance was tomorrow night, yes?

MARGERY: I thought, perhaps, perhaps I'd ask my brother to establish contact with your mother. I know mothers and sons sometimes have private things they'd like to say to each other. And rest assured, Mr. Carrington, I have a similar treat for you.

HOUDINI: I'm sure you are a very kind person, Mrs. Crandon. Perhaps I'm being overly suspicious, but do you know what a cynic might say about your invitation?

MARGERY: You'll have to tell me, Mr. Houdini. I'm afraid I have no idea how a cynic would think.

HOUDINI: Divide and conquer, Mrs. Crandon, divide and conquer.

MARGERY: I'll give you an alternative explanation. A good hostess likes to please her guests and not bore the others with conversations that won't interest them.

HOUDINI: Your husband and Hereward, they have no objections?

> [*Crandon and Carrington nod their agreement.*]

For many years, to talk with my mother, it is what I have wanted.

CRANDON: Carrington, in my library I have a humidor filled with some of Cuba's finest cigars. Perhaps you'd like to sample one? And then, of course, you could browse my books on spiritualism.

> [*With brandy glass in one hand, and taking along the decanter of bandy in the other, Crandon exits with Carrington.*]

MARGERY: Now, if you'll forgive me, I too must leave you for a short time so that I can prepare myself.

> [*Margery exits. Houdini gets up, runs his hand underneath the table and knocks on each of the table legs to see if any of them is hollow. Next he checks every object in the room, paying particular attention to the candelabra. After that, he picks up the chair on which Margery had been sitting, turns it over and carefully checks the underneath side. Before he can put it down, Margery enters, barefoot and wearing a semi-transparent negligee.*]

MARGERY; No strings, my dear Houdini, no balloons, no noise makers. You see, I have nothing to hide.

HOUDINI: So many try to hide, Mrs Crandon.

> [*Margery lights the candelabra and then turns off the electric lights. The two of them sit down across from each other and hold hands. The candelabra light only illuminates the lower part of their faces to their eyebrows and their eyes are in shadow.*]

FRED (V.O): I'm going to make you happy, Houdini.

HOUDINI: You are? I'm glad to hear that. But perhaps you could introduce yourself.

FRED (V.O.): Margery's my little sister. I'm Fred.

HOUDINI: And how are you going to make me happy, Fred?

FRED(V.O.): By bringing you a message from your mother.

HOUDINI: Can't bring my mother to speak to me? It would be marvelous to hear her voice again.

FRED(V.O.): No, I'm afraid I can't do that. Margie's only a medium for me. No one else.

HOUDINI: That is too bad. I'm sure you are a charming a person. But my mother you are not.

FRED(V.O.): For some reason she calls you Erik.

HOUDINI: The name she gave me when I was born. My name for the stage did not please her. What does she say?

FRED(V.O.): She wants you to know that, even though you didn't become a doctor, she's very proud of what you have accomplished. And she very much wants you to try harder to find a way for you to speak with her without using other spirits' mediums.

HOUDINI: Friedelicha, bei mir bist du shane.

FRED(V.O.): Come again?

HOUDINI: Du bist shane, Friedelicha, zehr shane.

FRED(V.O.): On the farm, we only spoke English.

HOUDINI: With my mother, it was only Yiddish. You see the problem, Fred.

FRED(V.0.): Now that your mother has crossed to another world, she talks with any other spirit in our own language, the one only spirits know.

HOUDINI: Is that so, Friedelicha? I had no idea.

END OF SCENE 11

Scene 12

Scene: *Crandon's bedroom. Crandon, wears reading glasses, and sits in silk pajamas propped up by pillows on a king sized bed. He reads a book as Margery enters. She still wears her negligee.*

CRANDON: And are our two guests happy?

MARGERY: You filled Mr. Carrington with enough brandy. Couldn't be happier. He's sleeping soundly in the guest bedroom down the hall.

CRANDON: And Houdini?

MARGERY: He's back at his hotel.

CRANDON: I take that to mean he's not happy.

MARGERY: He's happy all right, but for the wrong reasons. He thinks he's on the verge of exposing me as a fraud, and that makes him very, very happy.

CRANDON: A fraud?

MARGERY: He's a clever man. Knows all the tricks.

CRANDON: Tricks? What tricks? You don't do tricks.

MARGERY: Of course I do. Come on Leroy, surely a smart man like you knew.

CRANDON: Knew what?

MARGERY: At this late date, do I have to say it? I guess I do. The whole seance thing is a trick.

FRED(V.O.): Once you're dead, you're dead.

> [*Crandon pulls off his glasses and gets out of bed and heads towards Margery.*]

CRANDON:

[*Stunned*]

Wait a minute. You mean there is no spirit, no Fred.

MARGERY: I mean there is no spirit, no Fred.

CRANDON: What have you done to me? What have you done?

> [*Crandon goes to grab Margery by the throat,
> but she ducts, grabs his arm, puts him in a
> hammerlock and slams him against the wall.*]

MARGERY: If you're goin' to go on slicing up patients you'll need this arm, so
calm down.

> [*Margery releases Crandon and steps back. He
> turns around to face her rubbing the arm that
> she grabbed. Then he breaks down sobbing.*]

You wanted contact with the spirit world. I gave you contact with the spirit
world. I figured you knew it was just a game to please you. Like playing doctor
and nurse. Looks like you didn't figure it out.

CRANDON:

[*Now under control.*]

You don't understand. It's so hard to shine among all those smart men. I
worked at it and worked at it. But here was something none of them had even
thought of. I wanted it so much that I didn't see.

MARGERY: Houdini figured it out. It's my fault. I laid a trap for myself. He spotted
it and sprung it. I thought I'd done a thorough research job on him, but I
missed something, something about his mother.

CRANDON: So because of your carelessness, he could say something about us
on stage during his act right here in Boston. Or he could talk to newspaper
reporters And he will say something, won't he?

MARGERY: Of course he will. These days it's what he lives for. Getting out of
trunks at the bottom of the East River seems to have lost its charm for him.

CRANDON: I'll be ruined. Humiliated.

MARGERY: Pull yourself together. The first step is figuring out where to go from here.

CRANDON:

[*His anger building*]

So now that you've managed to throw me into the river, so to speak, what do you think will become of you? Before I go down, it would be nice to find out how well you swim on your own.

MARGERY: And before you get any bright ideas, divorcing your third wife won't get you nearly as much sympathy as a stiff upper lip.

CRANDON: Are you telling me I might as well give up now? Just let everything I care about come crashing down.

MARGERY: No. We can still save this. Notice I said we. What I have to do is put on a convincing performance that goes beyond the voice of Fred.

CRANDON: If Fred didn't fool him, what makes you think adding something else will?

MARGERY: Houdini is probably hopeless. Forget him. But don't forget Carrington. He's the key to our trunk at the bottom of the river. If he says he believes what he sees and Houdini says he doesn't, we won't win the prize. We won't be ruined either.

CRANDON: So, even if Houdini yells loudly, we're covered.

MARGERY: He'll have his facts and we'll have ours. We sell the idea that it's an honest difference of opinion between experts.

CRANDON:

[*Warming to the idea*]

And everyone who matters knows Houdini's a presumptuous over-the-hill Jew-boy. I bet he only became a judge in this contest to boost his escape artist career that's headed downhill. Like the rest of his greedy tribe, all he cares about is money.

MARGERY: He can't make money if he loses his reputation.

CRANDON: So, if Fred isn't enough, what else is there?

MARGERY: You'll see tomorrow, but here's what's important. When we sit down for the seance, be sure you sit on my right and don't grip my hand too tightly.

CRANDON: And tomorrow the spirits will be willing?

MARGERY: And tomorrow the spirits will be willing.

CRANDON: And Carrington will be willing?

MARGERY: Let's put it this way. With the hangover he'll undoubtedly have thanks to your brandy, I don't think detailed observation will be his strong suit.

> [*Margery removes her negligee and climbs into bed. After a bit of hesitation, Crandon follows.*]

END OF SCENE 12

Scene 13

Scene: *Library at the Crandon house.Crandon and Houdini enter. Crandon offers Houdini a chair and then sits at right angles to him so that the seat directly across from Houdini is vacant.*

CRANDON: My wife and Carrington will we along shortly.

HOUDINI: At the bottom of the East River, I learned patience. People say I am known for my patience.

CRANDON: Whatever the reason, being well known is very important to you, isn't it?

HOUDINI: I am an entertainer. Why hide from the public?

CRANDON: I'm sure you realize that when you discover that my wife is a genuine medium, you'll only enhance your reputation.

HOUDINI: Of course, of course. But, then, finding the opposite will do the same.

CRANDON: My Margery's genuineness will certainly be better for your reputation than continually discovering frauds. The public will get bored if you make too many of those announcements.

HOUDINI: Can you tell me how many is too many?

CRANDON: Are you implying that you have already decided that my wife is a fraud, a fake, without seeing a full seance? What reason could she have for faking

HOUDINI: The one who wins this prize can live on it for a year.

CRANDON:

> [*Gestures toward the wall to ceiling shelves filled with books.*]

As you can see, she lives very well and she never charges money for her services.

HOUDINI: When does anyone have enough money?

CRANDON: I will grant you the prize is enough money to tempt an ordinary person. But you see, when we win, we won't accept the prize money. We'll give it away.

HOUDINI: It is good to be rich.

CRANDON: Now that I think of it, perhaps it would be only fair to give the money to you. Surely you must have cancelled performances so that you could come here and act a contest judge.

HOUDINI: Only in Buffalo. Dr. Crandon, while I'm sure you are an honest man, some people might think you use the prize money as a bribe.

CRANDON: Well then, what if the winnings went to your favorite charity?

HOUDINI: People would still talk. And my reputation could suffer.

CRANDON: Shakespeare said it best: "He that robs me of my good name, makes me poor indeed."

HOUDINI:
"He that filches from me my good name
Robs me of that which enriches not him
And makes me poor indeed."

[*Crandon looks surprised, then angry.*]

HOUDINI: I know. A little Yid like me isn't supposed to know Shakespeare. In New York they put John Barrymore and me on the same bill. From the wings, night after night, I got to hear him do Iago. Now that I think of it, quoting from a character who lied all the time does you no good.

[*Crandon starts to say something, but just
then Margery enters. She's in her negligee and
sits down across from Houdini. She carries a
megaphone and a small wooden box. She places*]

*the large black megaphone on the table in front
of her with the wide opening face down. It has
several strips of luminescent paint circling the very
bottom and the very top. Margery then puts down
the small wooden box next to the megaphone.
Looking hungover, but with a weak smile on his
face, Carrington slowly enters and sits in the
vacant chair on Margery's left. Crandon sits on
her right and Houdini sits across from her. As
soon as he does, the lights go out and only the
glowing megaphone remains visible.*]

FRED(V.O.):

[The voice seems to come from the megaphone.]

There was a young man from New York
That the whole world would come to hail
And the mediums came as a lark
But he tried to put salt on their tale.

He salted them without a doubt
Oh so very happy was he.
And now if he has his way
He'll put salt all over me.

*[The table begins to bang on the floor and a bell
in the box then begins to ring. At the same time,
a coo-coo clock outside the room also begins to
sound. At this point, the megaphone jumps into
the air and pauses with the wide side pointing
down over Margery.]*

FRED(V.O.): Where do you want it Houdini?

HOUDINI: How about on the table, in front of me?

*[The megaphone flips down in front of Houdini
and lands with the wide side down.]*

FRED(V.O.): Good-bye Houdini.

[*The lights come on.*]

MARGERY: Leroy and I will leave you two gentleman to your discussions. When you're done, ring for the maid and she'll show you out. I'm sure you can do that yourselves. No need to summon spirits to ring for you.

[*Margery and Crandon exit.*]

HOUDINI: Nice little show. Short, clever.

CARRINGTON: Show? You think Margery just put on a show.

HOUDINI: You don't?

CARRINGTON: I'm not a fool, Houdini. I came into the room slowly because I was checking for wires or thread. There was none, at least none that I could see. Are you going to tell me, you found some?

HOUDINI: No, no wire, no thread, but a show is a show.

CARRINGTON: Without strings or wires, how does the bell in the box ring?

[*The bell in the box sounds. At first Carrington looks startled. Then he smiles.*]

CARRINGTON: And the coo-coo clock?

HOUDINI: Is it beyond belief that the sound of a ringing bell and the sound of a coo-coo are made by the person who also sounds like Fred?

CARRINGTON: The megaphone was no voice trick.

HOUDINI: But a trick it was.

[*With one hand, Houdini flips the megaphone onto his head, then with his head he flips it in front of Carrington.*]

HOUDINI: Want to know the man who met every fake medium at every county fair in Nebraska? You already do. Me. I know all their tricks. I did all the tricks.

CARRINGTON: Just because you can do what happened here doesn't mean Margery did what you did. The spirit of Fred could have done all those things.

HOUDINI: So could the real Margery.

CARRINGTON: But why would she? If she charged ten dollars a person to see her contact spirits, if she sold stories to newspapers or magazines, I'd lean in your direction. Do she and her husband even need money? Doesn't look like it to me.

HOUDINI: Would lightning strike this Jew-boy if I said money isn't everything?

CARRINGTON: If this is some convoluted plot of theirs, why did Sir Arthur put the Crandons' names forward to the editors of Scientific America first and told them about it afterwards? Does that sound like the way fakes would behave?

HOUDINI: Why do they do what they do? I don't know. Maybe for their own amusement.

CARRINGTON: That's not good enough for me.

HOUDINI: No more arguing. We just waste time. Let's settle this.

CARRINGTON: Then what do you propose?

HOUDINI: To show you they are fakes.

CARRINGTON: And how do you plan to do that?

HOUDINI: Patience, patience.

END OF SCENE 13

Scene 14

Scene: *Crandon dining room. Margery sitting in her negligee and Crandon paces around the room.*

CRANDON: This is a big mistake.

MARGERY: It's a gamble. Like poker. They raised. We've seen them. We didn't fold. Maybe they will.

CRANDON: But that's the point. We don't have to do anything at all. Why play a hand when you don't have to?

MARGERY: Of course you're right. We're bluffing. We do have to. If we don't, we lose Carrington.

CRANDON: But last time they were here, didn't it look like one said yes and the other one said no. That's the result we wanted, isn't it?

MARGERY: It wasn't just Houdini who asked for this one last session. Both of them did. If we refused, Carrington might have wavered.

CRANDON: I thought you said Carrington was a sure thing.

MARGERY: Houdini's kept him away. I haven't seen or talked to him in two weeks. I have no idea what he's thinking today.

CRANDON: Okay. I guess there's no avoiding it. You're prepared? Everything's arranged?

MARGERY: Prepared and arranged.

> [*Crandon continues pacing, but stops when he hears a knock on the door.*]

CRANDON: Enter!

[The door opens and Houdini and Carrington enter carrying a large wooden box between them. The box has hinges so that the front can be opened. It has a hole at the top large enough for someone's neck to fit in comfortably and it has arm holes on each side. The box has no bottom. The two men place the bottomless box over an empty chair.]

CRANDON: What in the world is that?

HOUDINI: A meeting place. A friendly spirit and a real medium can talk here, maybe share a corned beef sandwich.

MARGERY: I take it you want me to sit in your box.

CARRINGTON: It's not that we doubt your spirit...

HOUDINI: Just me.

CRANDON: If you are going to be rude to my wife, I shall ask you to leave.

HOUDINI: If you don't want to continue...

MARGERY: You'll go and tell the world.

HOUDINI: You choose.

CRANDON: Now you're threatening us. I won't have it.

CARRINGTON: Perhaps we'd better leave.

MARGERY: No, stay, stay. Of course I can't guarantee how my brother's spirit will react to finding me boxed up. He could become quite angry. But we shall see.

HOUDINI: Maybe I should be glad you don't talk to my mother. Now she, she knew how to get angry.

[Houdini makes a motion toward the box and Margery gets up and goes towards it. Carrington opens up the box and Margery sits in it. He

then closes the box and locks it in a place where Margery cannot reach.]

CARRINGTON: Are you comfortable Margery?

MARGERY: Yes, quite. It was kind of you to provide cushions.

HOUDINI: Now, one more thing, like home, the lights must stay on.

MARGERY: Fred's spirit has been in darkness for so many years that he can't deal with too much light. The candelabra would be the most he could tolerate.

HOUDINI: There is light and there is light. We can turn it out, if you insist.

MARGERY: Fred would find it more comforting.

[*Houdini pulls three phosphorescent strips of cloth from his pocket and proceeds to wrap and tie one around Margery's forehead and the other two around her wrists. Houdini then goes the back of the box where Margery is seated and comes back with a megaphone. He places it on the table in front of Margery.*]

CRANDON: You are a miserable cur, Houdini, a miserable cur.

[*The lights go out and only the strips tied to Margery are visible.*]

HOUDINI: Now, if Fred would be so kind, the megaphone in front of me, just like the last time.

[*Nothing happens.*]

FRED(V.O.): A little song is what I'll sing tonight, ...

HOUDINI: But not when the lights are on.

[*The lights go on.*]

CRANDON: You're a dead man Houdini, a dead man.

END OF SCENE 14

Scene 15

Scene: *Crandon's dining room. Margery sits on the sofa with a half full glass of whiskey on the end table in front of her and a bottle of whiskey next to the glass. She looks a good deeal older and her clothes are rumpled and look well worn. She hears a soft knock at the door.*

MARGERY: What is it now?

EVELYN:

> [*From off stage*]

> Margery. It's me, Evelyn. I knocked on the front door. No one answered, so I took a chance you just didn't hear and came in. Didn't mean to startle you.

MARGERY : Evey! Sorry thought it was that maid of mine pestering me about her money. It's been forever. Come in. Have a seat. Have a drink.

> [*Evelyn enters and sits on the sofa with Margery.*]

EVELYN: A bit early for me.

MARGERY: Well not early for me. I know why you're here, right?

EVELYN: I guess you do. Must be hard on you. He died suddenly? Without any warning?

MARGERY: I guess I wasn't all that surprised.

EVELYN: I'm sorry. Mark wouldn't come with me. I know what happened wasn't your fault.

MARGERY: No need to apologize. Mark and Leroy haven't talked to each other for what? Ten years? Never made up. No reason for him to be here now.

EVELYN: That Houdini nonsense. Do you know why Leroy kept going on and on all those years about Houdini? Couldn't he just move on?

MARGERY: He thought Houdini ruined his life.

EVELYN: But Houdini never said a word about Leroy that I know of. It was you he defamed.

MARGERY: Leroy felt it more than I did. He had such plans.

EVELYN: Houdini said you were a fake, not Leroy. If that isn't defaming you, I don't know what is.

MARGERY: Houdini and I were in a contest. He won. That's what bothered Leroy. As he put it, that jumped up Jew-boy beat the Back Bay doctor and his wife. And he couldn't stand the humiliation.

EVELYN: But Houdini died just a little more than a year after that Scientific American contest. Leroy hung on to that grudge all these years. It makes no sense.

> [*Margery pours herself another stiff drink and gulps down about half. Evelyn gives her a questioning look.*]

MARGERY: Do you know how Houdini died?

EVELYN: Didn't his appendix burst or some such thing.

> [*Margery takes another drink.*]

MARGERY: Leroy and I killed him.

EVELYN:

> [*Horrified*]

What? You didn't! What do you mean? You were here in Boston when he died some place else.

MARGERY: Detroit. He died in Detroit. We never meant to kill him. We only wanted to embarrass him.

EVELYN: How could you do that?

MARGERY: Make him cancel a show. Maybe even force him to stop in the middle of a performance. Make him look bad, over-the-hill.

EVELYN: How's that supposed to help the two of you?

MARGERY: Leroy had this crazy idea that if he discredited Houdini, I could make a comeback. And if I did, he did.

EVELYN: Sounds like nonsense to me. Did you believe things would go that way?

MARGERY: Not really, but Leroy did.

EVELYN: I still don't see how you could disable Houdini from here.

[*Margery finishes her drink and pours another.*]

MARGERY: That's where Joshua came in. Do you remember him?

EVELYN: Joshua? Vaguely. Young man. Did some gardening. Did repairs for you.

MARGERY: Sweet Joshua was strong. So strong. Leroy gave him money to look for a chance to punch Houdini in the stomach. I'm sure he didn't mean to kill him. Joshua was such a sweet boy.

EVELYN:

[*Stunned*]

He doesn't sound very sweet to me.

MARGERY:

[*Downs her drink.*]

Leroy wouldn't let him come back after Detroit. Never the same after that. Now Leroy's dead too and none of it matters any more to anyone.

EVELYN: Not anyone except you.

MARGERY: Except me.

EVELYN: What are you going to do now?

MARGERY: I don't know. There's not much money left.

EVELYN: I guess it's not too late to go back to what you were doing before you got married.

MARGERY: Once upon a time, many years ago, I was a magician, a very good magician. I wonder if there's any more magic left in the world.

> [*Raises her glass in a silent toast and then drains the glass.*]

END OF PLAY

EDUCATING HENRY ADAMS

CHARACTERS:

Henry Adams
Clover Adams
John La Farge
Lizzy Cameron
Marau

Trigger Warning:
A suicide takes place.

Prologue

Scene: *In an otherwise dark stage, a spotlight comes up on HENRY ADAMS face and then expands to show all of him.*

HENRY: I feel it necessary to introduce myself. I am Henry Adams. I've been dead for over a century. In my day, I was at least as well known as Alexander Hamilton.

For this first appearance, so-called experts advised me to surround myself with an artificial, ghostly fog. As you can see, I refused. I've always valued clarity and education far above artificiality.

In pursuit of those goals I offer a brief view my life. Award-winning Harvard history professor. Well-read non-fiction and fiction author. Respected observer of the American political scene.

Of course while I lived my life, I saw no reason to brag. I felt like a ponderous gadfly.

Worse. Three women in my life mattered most to me. All of them rightfully considered me clueless.

Yet, to my surprise, they didn't exit laughing. Instead, each in her own way tried to educate me. You are about to see if they succeeded.

Act 1,
Scene 1

Scene: *Living room of Adams house in Washington D.C. It has comfortable chairs and couch. A large landscape painting hangs over the fire place mantle. CLOVER ADAMS sits on the couch with a large 1880s camera on the coffee table in front of her. She adjusts various settings on the camera. The telephone rings. HENRY enters and picks it up.*

HENRY: Hello. John good of you to call. [*pause*] No. Shouldn't take you long from the station.

[*Hangs up. To Clover.*]

As you call tell. John. On his way. He probably needs to see the wall completely bare where we're going to put his portrait of you.

[*Henry takes a nearby step ladder to the front of the mantle and starts to remove the picture that hangs there.*]

CLOVER: My darling Henry. Please don't. I have this horror of blank space.

HENRY: You've never mentioned it before.

CLOVER: One of my many secrets.

HENRY: Still, horror seems a bit extreme. When you're lying there your bed every night, I presume at some point you stare at the blank ceiling. I certainly do at mine.

[*Henry finishes removing the picture, gets of the step ladder, and puts the picture to one side.*]

CLOVER: It's not the same. The blank space you just created will keep saying, "Fill me. Fill me. Fill me up." It reminds me of having a blank mind.

HENRY: Dearest Clover, you could call it a resting mind.

CLOVER: By whatever term, after my mind does it, I feel like I've lost control. It might wander anywhere.

HENRY: Sort of the thinking person's equivalent of idle hands and the devil's workshop.

CLOVER: Perhaps, I should use my hands, to at least temporarily fill that blank space with a suitably enlarged and framed picture of my father.

HENRY: If you like. But John assures me, once he's completed his sketch, your portrait won't take long.

> [*Before Clover can reply, there is a brief knock at the door and LIZZIE CAMERON bursts in. She is a young, attractive blond, in her late twenties. She dresses expensively, but informally, in the latest fashion.*]

LIZZY: Help!

HENRY: I'll guess. Your married cook maid has run off with your married butler.

CLOVER: And the maid has left with a bun in the oven and you don't know what to do.

HENRY: So you need the name of a good employment agency this minute.

LIZZY:
> [*Laughs and shakes her head.*]

You two! Mother's coming tomorrow.

HENRY: Hopefully you're not asking us to man the barricades. My guess is we'll have no better luck keeping her out than the Confederates had in keeping your Uncle William and his soldiers out of Georgia.

CLOVER: Is she planning on staying with you?

LIZZY: One of the few things Don and I agree on is trying to keep my mother at a safe distance. She'll stay with Uncle John.

HENRY: So what kind of help did you have in mind?

LIZZY: This Saturday we're expected to join the two of them for a play in Uncle John's box at Ford's theater.

HENRY: One evening certainly seems more bearable than sharing meals for a week.

LIZZY: Only on the surface.

CLOVER: So take us below.

LIZZY: Don will undoubtedly appear at theater well fortified with liquid courage for combat. He'll hurl himself at mother through any available breach. Of course, stone cold sober, she'll hurl herself right back at him.

HENRY: And bodies will cover the floor.

CLOVER: So. You'd like the two of us to come along and subtly fill the breach.

LIZZY: Yes. Please. An act of friendship I'll appreciate till my dying day.

CLOVER: I'm happy to throw myself into your dreaded breach.

HENRY: Speaking of friends and breaches, I saw that Henry V is at Ford's. There's already been one assassination there. Nice to think we can prevent a second.

LIZZIE: You have no idea how on target your comment is.

CLOVER: Do tell. I mean you to take that remark literally.

LIZZIE: My ever aspiring uncle, Senator John Sherman, would like to world to think of him as future President John Sherman.

HENRY: He didn't.

LIZZIE: He did.

CLOVER: Bought the box where Lincoln sat when John Wilkes made his unfortunate appearance.

HENRY: And then we have the unfortunate coincidence that his brother, Edmund, plays Henry V.

CLOVER: At least, unlike John, he's already waving a sword and won't be jumping on the stage, gun still in hand.

> [*JOHN LAFARGE appears at the open door. He has a sketch pad in one hand. A series of colored pencils stick out of the top pocket of his artist's smock. He dresses in the stereotypical outfit of a Romantic era artist, complete with beret.*]

JOHN: Maid let me in. This still a good time?

LIZZY:

> [*Heads for the door. To Clover and Henry*]

Thank you. Thank you. Thank you both. [*To John*] Nice to see you. We must just chat sometime.

> [*Lizzy hurries out. Henry and Clover look at each other and then break out laughing.*]

JOHN: Who or what was that?

CLOVER: Hurricane Lizzy. And John assured me we were moving into one of Washington's quieter neighborhoods.

HENRY: My love, I don't think the terms, Lizzie, and quiet will ever belong in the same sentence.

CLOVER: She puts on a performance as good as anything we're likely to see at Ford's.

HENRY: Do you think she's performing?

CLOVER: Perhaps a bit. But she's so lovely, I'm willing to overlook it.

HENRY: I think she's clever. And perfectly genuine. All right. That will be my exit line. I'll leave the two of you to work at filling up that blank space on the wall.

[*Henry exits. John has an inaudible conversation with Clover that leads her to pose for him standing next to her camera that she mounts on a tripod. He motions her to try various poses and finally settles for one in which Clover holds the cabled shutter release and faces him. He starts sketching her.*]

CLOVER: John, how much is Henry paying you for my portrait?

JOHN: Think of all the cliches you've ever heard about not telling and pick one of them as my answer.

CLOVER: I am willing to give you a signed blank personal check. You could, privately, fill in double the fee Henry promised you. Then both of us could forget about the portrait.

JOHN: Looks like you need an early break.

[*Clover goes over to a sofa and sits down.*]

CLOVER: I've got another camera. You could take my picture. Then I wouldn't have to stand there forever while you stare at my face and put it on that piece of paper of yours.

JOHN: I don't know the first thing about cameras.

CLOVER: Good.

JOHN: Good?

CLOVER: My father was a great teacher of many things. I've always wanted a quiet opportunity to follow in his footsteps. Now you've given me the opportunity to do it out of the limelight.

JOHN: Thank you for your kind offer.

[*As he finishes his statement, to emphasize the point, he gives an exaggerated formal bow.*]

CLOVER: But you're turning it down.

JOHN: I don't mean to sound like someone from the previous century, but I feel mechanical aid and art are a poor mix.

CLOVER: If I close my eyes, I can see you in a powdered wig.

JOHN: The thing is, today's cameras reduce everything to black and white.

CLOVER: You could take notes on the colors.

JOHN: To my mind, if I don't begin by using color, the completed portrait becomes nothing more than an act of my imagination. Not a true image of you.

CLOVER: I can prove to you that you're underrating photography.

JOHN: Here's where I prove to you I don't belong in a powdered wig. I'd be happy to look at your proof.

> [*Clover gets up and goes to a table. She pulls out a drawer and takes a photograph album from it. She opens the album and motions to John. He comes over, and they sit side by side and go through it together.*]

JOHN: I take it you have a reason for photographing all those lovely pictures of the same man.

CLOVER: He's my father.

JOHN: You show him with love and care. Impressive pictures.

CLOVER:

> [*Gets up.*]

Then it's settled. John, come over here to the camera and I'll show you how to time your exposure.

JOHN: But it's not just the lack of color that bothers me.

> [*Disappointed, Clover sits down.*]

CLOVER: I can see that wig on your head again.

JOHN: Pictures taken with a camera, even your lovely ones, only show the outside of your subject. I can't paint from that.

CLOVER: I'm sure in your art classes you studied anatomy and know very well what's on the inside.

JOHN: I mean your character. Who you are, really.

CLOVER: In that case, I'll repeat my offer of the check. But triple the amount.

JOHN: I am slowly getting the idea that you don't want me to paint your portrait.

CLOVER: Mr. La Farge, you are a very perceptive man.

JOHN: And would it make a difference if my name was Whistler or Sargent?

CLOVER: No.

JOHN: That leaves just one possibility.

CLOVER: And that is?

JOHN: I'll bet you think all people who sit for portraits end up with lifeless two dimensional images of themselves.

CLOVER: You'll lose money on your bet.

JOHN: Okay. I give up.

CLOVER: You gave me the reason. Your portrait will turn me inside out.

JOHN: Doesn't Henry want to put your portrait right here in this room? Only Henry and your closest friends will see it.

CLOVER: I don't want them to.

JOHN: And I would have thought those are the people you'd most want to see who you really are. That is, of course, presuming I get you right.

CLOVER : With your talent, I'm sure you will.

JOHN: I suppose I should feel extra special because you think I'm so insightful.

CLOVER: Yes, you should.

JOHN: I can't believe that you think that there's something so terrible inside of you that it needs hiding.

CLOVER: We all have secrets.

JOHN: Well, if you're really backing out, I leave it to you to tell Henry.

CLOVER: I guess he does need to know.

JOHN: He will most certainly ask me why I'm returning his money.

CLOVER:

> [*Sighs, stands and picks up the shutter release.*]

I presume you want me to stand in the same place.

END OF SCENE 1

Scene 2

Scene: *John La Farge's artist studio in New York. La Farge works on a large table. He has several easels spread around the room, some with partially finished aintings on them. Henry enters.*]

JOHN: Henry! I wasn't expecting you.

HENRY: Historical Society meeting here in New York. I'm on my way back to Washington. Thought I'd stop by to pick-up Clover's portrait.

JOHN: You didn't have to do that. I'm headed your way at the end of the week.

> [*John goes over to a pile of finished paintings, pulls Clover's from the stack. He holds up her portrait for Henry to see and then puts it on an easel. Henry examines it closely and nods approvingly. But then he frowns.*]

HENRY: Of course with Clover, what'll please her at any given moment can be a bit of a guessing game.

JOHN: At any given moment?

HENRY: Her mood can suddenly plummet and then nothing pleases her.

JOHN: I'd like to make a self-interested recommendation.

HENRY: Go ahead.

JOHN: Hide her portrait. Pull it out when she's in the right mood. So I don't have to start from scratch again.

HENRY:

> [*Begins to fidget with the placement of Clover's portrait on the easel.*]

While we're on the subject of pleasing Clover.

[*John cuts in.*]

JOHN: A topic on which I'm sure you're an expert.

HENRY; If only.

[*Pause*]

What I want to ask.

[*Fidgets more. Pauses again.*]

Please promise me it will stay just between us.

JOHN: Of course.

HENRY: Any embarrassment 'll be on my side.

JOHN: Embarrassment?

HENRY : You're the expert here. You know more about married life than I do.

JOHN: No need for embarrassment. I presume you want to know how to balance your working life and keep both a wife and children happy. Well, to begin with...

[*Henry cuts him short.*]

HENRY: Not exactly. With my wife. With Clover. How to... How to...

JOHN: What then? Out with it!

HENRY: It's just that... That is to say... We have never... We've never...

JOHN: Oh. Oh my.

HENRY: It's probably my fault.

JOHN: Why do you say that?

HENRY: Look at what's standing in front of you.

JOHN: One of the most renowned scholars in America. Admired by everyone who matters. Famous the world over.

HENRY: A short bald man. One who speaks to both women and men in the same off-putting way. Clover or any woman, for that matter, can't possibly find that appealing.

JOHN: She did marry you.

HENRY: I think her father told her it was time.

JOHN: She must have found something about you appealing.

HENRY: We do have the same jaundiced view of today's politics and politicians.

JOHN: Not very romantic, I must say.

HENRY: I can assure you it isn't.

JOHN: Aren't there other things that bring the two of you close?

HENRY: Do you mean physically close?

JOHN: Let's start there.

HENRY: Not very promising, I'm afraid.

JOHN: Why not?

HENRY: To begin with, we sleep in separate bedrooms.

JOHN: You're joking.

HENRY: She goes to bed earlier than I do. Obviously the kind thing to do is not to wake her by turning on lights, climbing into the bed.

JOHN: I think you know what you're killing with kindness.

HENRY: Clover seemed relieved. She kissed the top of my head when she thanked me for suggesting it.

JOHN: And did it occur to you to kiss her back? On the lips.

HENRY:
[*Puzzled*]

Well, no.

JOHN: Don't you ever want to get to know her in what I will call politely the Biblical sense?

HENRY: Of course I want to know Clover in the Biblical sense. As you put it. That's why I'm asking for your advice.

JOHN: Take the initiative.

HENRY: I'm not a rapist, John. If Clover doesn't want to, then we don't.

JOHN: Doesn't that strike you as odd? At the very least.

HENRY: Precisely. And your advice is?

JOHN: There must be things that will bring you close to each other. Mutual interests.

HENRY: I do find all aspects her picture making fascinating. Especially the way she develops them in her dark room.

JOHN: Standing together in a smelly room filled with chemicals probably won't do.

HENRY: She doesn't only take pictures of her father, you know. She does take the occasional one of me.

JOHN: In the nude?

[*Henry just glares at him.*]

JOHN: All right then. How about the obvious. Ask her what the trouble is.

HENRY: We've never talked of such matters. We just smile at one another and go our own way.

JOHN: I'll tell you something that will surprise you.

HENRY: Surprise away.

JOHN: Henry, from my perspective, you should be my model.

HENRY: Now don't make a joke of this.

JOHN: I'm not. My difficulties are the reverse of yours. With Betsy and me, the children keep making their yearly appearances.

HENRY: I guess if you're looking for ways to discourage a woman, I am the ideal model.

JOHN: Right. Betsy and I should try separate bedrooms.

HENRY: Maybe you should travel far, far away.

JOHN:

[*Laughs*]

I hear Tahiti is very nice this time of year.

HENRY: Right. There I solved your problem. Now solve mine.

JOHN:

[*Pauses, looks doubtful.*]

Okay. I've got what's going to sound like a strange suggestion.

HENRY: Strange can be good.

JOHN:

[*Gathers himself together, clears his throat.*]

Tell me, Henry, when you taught at Harvard, did your students teach you anything?

HENRY; They did.

JOHN: That's why you need to find a way for Clover to become a teacher.

HENRY: Who's she supposed to teach?

JOHN: A younger woman.

HENRY: You're losing me.

JOHN: She should teach a young woman how to become an adult, child-bearing woman.

HENRY: You've got quite a sense of humor.

JOHN: You must know. She's really keen to teach. Find a way to put her together with a young woman. It'll happen naturally.

HENRY: I can see it now. The advertisement in the newspapers. Wanted: a young woman to learn the facts of life from a teacher who wants to avoid them.

JOHN: I'll ignore the sarcasm. Seriously. Think about the the young women you two know.

HENRY: All right, I'm thinking.

JOHN: I will bet there's one who's motherless. Or one who doesn't get on with her mother.

HENRY: Our neighbor, Lizzy Cameron. You met her. Lizzy's mother has a mentality rather like with her brother. General Sherman. The one who burned down Atlanta.

JOHN: I remember Lizzy. Gorgeous. Fascinating. Unforgettable.

HENRY: And married to the aged, often drunken Senator Cameron. She could use a sympathetic ear.

JOHN: Married. She won't work.

HENRY: I don't see why not.

JOHN: I doubt that she needs the kind of education you want Clover to give out.

HENRY: All right. There's Anne Morgan. Her father says he's often at wits end. Hasn't a clue what to tell her about the world she'll face as a married woman.

JOHN: Her mother?

HENRY: A suicide, I fear.

JOHN: Unfortunate for them. Ideal for you.

HENRY: I take you're not asking me to tell Clover she should teach Anne how to be a woman.

JOHN: Of course not. Very quietly, find a way to put Anne and Clover together. Then you'll see if she's talented enough to teach Clover what you want her to know.

END OF SCENE 2

Scene 3

Scene: *Clover stands in a hallway outside Henry's study. She holds a letter in one hand. She takes a deep breath and enters the study.*

Henry sits at his desk, working on book proofs. Clover gives him a quick kiss on the top of his head. They smile at one another and Clover sits in a comfortable arm chair.

CLOVER: I'm going up to see my father and open the summer house a couple of weeks early.

HENRY: I've got these blasted appointments, so....

[*Clover cuts in.*]

CLOVER: I know. Come when you can. I'll ask Lizzie to look in on you.

HENRY: You know I hate it when you travel on your own.

CLOVER: It's necessary.

[*Henry briefly stops editing, and gives Clover a concerned look, then brightens up.*]

HENRY: But next week we've the reunion of our little group here. You've spent the last few days saying how much you're looking forward to seeing them.

CLOVER: It's been a while.

HENRY: Think of what you're missing. Tall tales, humorous encounters, all the best gossip.

[*Henry looks at Clover expectantly.*]

CLOVER: Not seeing them will make me sad. But I have to go.

HENRY: Making you sad, my love, is the last thing I want.

CLOVER: I know. I know.

HENRY: So tell me why you must go now.

> [*Clover gets up and hands Henry the letter. He glances at it, and then goes back to concentrating on his proofs.*]

HENRY: Your father sounds like his usual self to me.

CLOVER: He says the usual things. But he's hiding something.

> [*Clover takes back the letter and goes back and sits in her chair.*]

HENRY: You two are so close. He tells you everything.

CLOVER: I can tell from the way he writes. He's trying to spare my feelings.

HENRY: Well maybe after all these years on his own, he's found a nice widow. Can't figure a way to let you know.

CLOVER: More likely he's ill.

HENRY: You're letting your womanly instincts and emotions overwhelm you.

> [*Clover give him a sharp look.*]

HENRY: Perhaps I should say daughterly instincts.

CLOVER: Let's say they guide me.

HENRY: It's all pure speculation on your part.

CLOVER: My darling, shall I be blunt?

HENRY: You usually don't ask permission.

CLOVER: You don't like it when I make decisions on my own.

HENRY: Now I'll be equally blunt. Even when we're together, I can see you fighting off melancholy.

CLOVER: And except for when we were on our honeymoon, I've won the battle.

HENRY: If you're right, coping with your sick father. It could tip you back over the edge.

CLOVER: I don't see how going a couple of weeks early will upset me or anyone else.

HENRY: My love, the whole time we're apart, I'll worry.

CLOVER: And how do you think I'll feel if I waited for you and something happened to him?

HENRY: If you go and treat him like he's ill, both you 'll end up upset. With each other.

CLOVER:

[*Smiling.*]

My darling Henry, I take it your instinct and emotion lead you to this conclusion.

HENRY:

[*With his index finger, Henry draws a one in the air, points to Clover and smiles back.*]

No. Experience. I can just see you constantly hovering about him.

CLOVER: My trick will be to hover invisibly.

HENRY: If he catches on, it 'll annoy him.

CLOVER: Sick people are always grouchy.

HENRY: If you annoy him now, he won't ask for your help when he really needs it.

CLOVER:

[*Pause*]

What if I ask Anne to come with me? She's so bright and spritely. She'd cheer anyone up.

HENRY: Well, I guess there's a chance that would work.

CLOVER: Then on your say-so, I'll take it.

HENRY: Someone not paying careful attention to our conversation would think this whole thing was my idea.

> [*Clover goes over to Henry, kisses him on the top of his head again and exits. Henry gives a big exhale and shakes his head.*]

END OF SCENE 3

Scene 4

Scene: *Lizzy sits on a day bed. A colorful scarf binds her long, blond hair tightly to her head. She wears a Japanese style silk dressing gown and matching slippers.*

Clover sits nearby on a nearby chair, dressed all in black. She has a box at her feet containing her camera and glass negatives. A folded tripod lays next to the box.

A teapot, cups, small plates and the remains of a cake are on a coffee table in front of the day bed. A vase filled with yellow roses is also on the table.

With her profile to the audience Clover sits at the narrow end of the table on the side closest to Lizzy,. Lizzy faces the front of the stage.

CLOVER: Of course, you've heard of would-be Senator Robson.

LIZZY: Indeed I have.

CLOVER: Well, after he failed to get a Senate seat, I heard him asked Mrs. Beale if she could think of a permanent place for him. Without a pause she said that for years the penitentiary had yearned for his presense.

[*Lizzy laughs.*]

And then, of course there's your uncle, Senator Sherman. I'm sure you've noticed. When he talks, he swallows his words. I call that a nice bit of compensation for him. No one else will swallow them.

[*Lizzy laughs again.*]

LIZZY: You always do this. Laughter may be the best medicine, but you're making my sides hurt.

CLOVER: When I make you laugh, I feel better.

LIZZY: You and your father were very close, weren't you?

CLOVER: After mother died in child-bed, he raised me. Ever so lovingly.

LIZZY: Given my family, I can only imagine.

CLOVER: After Henry and I first married, my father and I saw each other every day. Then we moved here. We bought a little cottage on the lake near his and still spent our summers together.

LIZZY: That must have been marvelous. My father got me out of the house as soon as possible. Married me off to the highest bidder.

CLOVER: I think fathers should give their daughters a sense of stability, set boundaries. Like mine did. On our own, it's so hard to figure out what instincts to follow.

LIZZY: After all you say about your father, I should've been the one to bring flowers.

CLOVER: I'm yours, heart and soul. They tell me that's what yellow roses say.

LIZZY: You and Henry 've always made me feel that way. With Don being what he is and away so much. The two of you. You're like a double bear hug.

CLOVER: When I heard you were ill, I didn't want you to feel that you're on your own.

LIZZY: With your father and all. It's so kind of you to come over.

CLOVER: It's important to let people know others care about them. While they're still here. While I'm still here.

LIZZY: You're sounding very pessimistic about life.

CLOVER: People have a way of vanishing unexpectedly. Like Anne.

LIZZY: Anne Morgan? Vanished?

CLOVER: From my life.

LIZZY: You've had a falling out?

CLOVER: She married an Englishman.

LIZZY:
                                        [Laughs]

It's not like she took poison.

CLOVER: Just this past summer, we lay on a blanket in the sunshine, played with each others hair and laughed and laughed. It seems like five thousand years ago.

LIZZY: I know it won't be the same, but...

[*Clover cuts her off.*]

CLOVER: She'll have children and die in childbirth.

LIZZY:

[*Lizzy looks shocked. She takes a moment to compose herself before she speaks.*]

I don't know what to say.

CLOVER: Before you vanish, I want to capture you just as you are.

[*Clover goes to her camera box. She takes out the camera, puts it on the tripod and points it toward Lizzy. Lizzy is momentarily surprised, but then begins to smooth her hair and her clothes.*]

No. Stop.
You must hold very still until I'm done. I'll count to three.

[*Lizzy tries to smile. It looks fake. Sensing the problem, she takes a slow breath and changes to looking serene. She feels more comfortable with the pose and lets out her breath. Clover looks into the camera viewer and puts her finger on the shutter release.*]

One. Two. Three!

[*She takes the glass negative out of the camera, shields it from light and puts another negative in the camera.*]

Again. One. Two. Three!

[*Repeats the process.*]

One last time. One. Two. Three!

[*Clover repeats the drill one more time. She closes the box and looks at Lizzy.*]

LIZZY: I hope you'll show Henry the pictures.

CLOVER: They're for Henry. You know he's in love with you.

LIZZY: I'm sure Henry cares for me. But love?

CLOVER: He doesn't realize it yet, but he's in love with you.

LIZZY: I'm sure men have their fantasies, including Henry. But they're usually about something much more basic than love.

CLOVER: With Henry, it's different.

LIZZY: I'm not sure what you want me to do with that information.

CLOVER: Show him the occasional kindness.

LIZZY: Have I ever been unkind to him?

CLOVER: You haven't given him the type of kindness he can't bring himself to ask you for.

LIZZY: Are you saying what I think you're saying?

CLOVER: It's the custom for New Englanders of my class to speak indirectly. I don't share it. Give him as much pleasure in bed as you can manage.

LIZZY: You're really asking me to sleep with your husband?

CLOVER: I've something more active in mind.

LIZZY: I don't know whether to be offended or flattered.

CLOVER: Flattered.

LIZZY: I hope so.

CLOVER: I'm sure you don't show that sort of kindness to all the men who hang about you.

LIZZY: Not if I have a choice.

CLOVER: I can see you admire Henry. You must know. He's caring. Gentle.

LIZZY: Of course. I have been on the receiving end.

CLOVER: Well then, offering Henry this kindness should be a rewarding experience. I know it's one he hasn't had.

LIZZY: Once again, I'm speechless.

CLOVER: Henry believes I'm fooled by my instincts and sentiments. I'm not.

LIZZY: If that's how he sees you, I wonder how he sees me?

CLOVER: As the undeclared love of his life.

LIZZY: And can you tell me what you think will prompt him to make that declaration.

CLOVER: He'll say what he has to say when the time is right for him. Dear man. He is so clueless.

> [*Clover gets up, packs up her camera
> equipment.*]

Good-bye Lizzy.

> [*As Clover leaves, she kisses Lizzy full on the lips
> and exits.*]

END OF SCENE 4

Scene 5

Scene: *Clover enters her darkroom. The light in it is red. Pictures hang on lines stretched around the room. Trays for developing negatives and prints cover the table located to the side of the stage. Shelves full of chemicals line the wall above the table. A butcher block like table stands in the center of the darkroom.*

Clover removes the pictures she has taken of Lizzy out of a white, enamel tray, holds them up one at a time as she looks at them. She uses wooden clothes pins to hang them on a nearby line.

After she finishes, Clover takes a bottle from a shelf, places on the butcher block and stares at it. She finally unscrews the top of the bottle and stares again. Clover then picks up the bottle.

END OF SCENE 5

Scene 6

Scene: *Henry and Lizzie sit bundled up in warm coats on a bench in front of the Clover Adams memorial in the Rock Creek Cemetery. The winged sculpted angel above the grave is behind them, center stage.*

LIZZIE: Perhaps it's time to find another way to remember her.

HENRY: I'd like to think she knows we're both here.

LIZZIE: But you don't really think she does.

HENRY: I don't.

LIZZIE: I've tried.

HENRY: To believe she knows?

LIZZIE: To make you feel better. Tried and failed.

HENRY: She was my wife. I should've taken better care of her.

LIZZIE: We all should've.

HENRY: Me. Most of all.

LIZZIE: Do you really think any of us could have stopped her?

HENRY: I've failed in everything that matters.

LIZZIE: It hurts me so much to see you torturing yourself like this.

HENRY: I just can't get beyond this feeling that more than my height comes up short.

LIZZIE: My father, my husband. They're genuine, no excuses, failures.

HENRY: That's harsh.

LIZZY: They destroy lives, the lives of the people they should love. You're not even close.

HENRY: If we don't count Clover.

LIZZY: Henry, why can't you take a compliment and not undermine it?

HENRY: Because the words "Henry" and "compliment" shouldn't appear in the same sentence.

LIZZY: Please don't make me sound insincere or manipulative.

HENRY: You can't think I meant to...

[*Lizzy cuts him off.*]

LIZZY: Why are you so determined to see yourself as a failure?

HENRY: Let's start with the obvious. Unlike other members of my family, I didn't become president of the United States.

LIZZY : Okay. Let's review.

HENRY: Review what?

LIZZY: Your place in the political world.

HENRY: Such as it is.

LIZZY: You're the man who thought President Grant and his friends corrupt. And said so loudly and often before hardly anyone else did.

HENRY: I pointed out the obvious.

LIZZY: And when the Republican Party, your party, sold its soul to the likes of Jay Gould and the other upstart tycoons, you were anything but quiet about that too.

HENRY: For all the good it did. Why bring all this up?

LIZZY: After all that, you're too smart a man to think the Republicans would nominate you for president.

HENRY: You just proved my point. Too clever by half, as the English put it.

LIZZY: If you still want to run for president here are your choices. Join with the party of rum, Romanism and rebellion. Or maybe found your own.

HENRY: And in the first case won't get nominated and in the second, I won't get elected. Does any of that make me any less of a failure?

LIZZY: It's the people you're calling out who should feel guilty, not you. You should feel proud of what you did. I'm proud of you for doing it.

HENRY: But lurking just below my surface, isn't there a kind of self-destructiveness?

LIZZY: It amazes me.

HENRY: What?

LIZZY: How your sense of family privilege and New England puritan guilt somehow manage to come together and overwhelm all your intelligence.

HENRY: All right. Let's leave my political failure to one side.

LIZZY: Happily.

HENRY: What I feel about my dead wife has nothing to do with my intelligence.

LIZZY: That leaves your instincts and emotions. The ones Clover told me you thought overwhelmed her.

HENRY: As they now overwhelm me.

LIZZY: Irony noted.

HENRY: I'll give you another one. In the grip of these feelings, I can still reach logical conclusions.

LIZZY: And the irony is that...

HENRY: That logic leads me to believe that logic isn't the be-all of human existence.

LIZZY: So you're abandoning reason to live a miserable life.

HENRY: What if I could use something other than reason to change my fate.

LIZZY: Use it.

HENRY:

> [*Henry straightens up and blurts out his feelings.*]

Can you do this friend a favor? Can you fall in love with me?

> [*Briefly, Lizzy looks surprised at what Henry has said. She turns toward him expectantly. He continues to sit there. Expectant, motionless. Lizzy sighs.*]

LIZZY: Henry, most men making such a declaration, would take me in their arms and kiss me passionately.

HENRY: Uninvited?

LIZZY: Uninvited.

HENRY: I don't know what I'd do if I tried and you didn't want me to.

LIZZY: Have you ever taken a woman in yours arms and kissed her passionately?

HENRY: Clover never wanted that.

LIZZY: Did you ever? Do you want to now?

HENRY: Perhaps sitting in front of Clover's memorial isn't the best place.

LIZZY: Close your eyes. Pretend we're standing in your bedroom.

HENRY: The two of us shouldn't be alone there.

LIZZY: Then a room of your choosing.

HENRY: Honestly. I don't know.

LIZZY: Clover predicted this would happen.

HENRY: That I wouldn't be able to kiss you passionately?

LIZZY: That one day you'd tell me you loved me.

HENRY: Here's the tragedy. She knew me better than I knew her.

LIZZY: Here's what I know about you, Henry. You're one of the most insightful people I've ever met. And you've treated me better than any man I've ever known.

HENRY: And that's what I want to keep on doing.

LIZZY: If I could cancel time for both of us and take us back, I'd come forward with you. I wouldn't hesitate for a minute. I wonder, even then, if you'd have done the same.

HENRY: Because now I hesitate.

LIZZY: Yes. That's you.

HENRY: My seemingly inescapable personal history.

LIZZY: I think it's time for you to wander. Go to a place that's as unlike here as you can imagine. When you get there, look for the piece of you that you've hidden from yourself.

HENRY: But right after Clover died, John and I went off to Japan.

LIZZY: You ran away to Japan to escape. Not to find.

HENRY: Even that didn't work. In the end both John and I came back frustrated.

LIZZY: Here's your chance to redeem yourselves.

HENRY: And if I do, what then?

LIZZY: Then we'll see. We'll see.

[Henry exits, stage left. Lizzy exits, stage left.]

END OF ACT 1

Act 2, Scene 1

Scene: *On stage left Henry sits at a desk in his ship's compartment. A porthole is above the desk. Lizzy sits at her desk, stage right, in front of French windows. As each one writes, their recorded voices say what they are writing.*

HENRY: The ship floats motionless on a calm sea. I still search for calm. I seek it for your sake. Life without attachment isn't worth living. Without my attachment to you, I have no reason to ever go home.

If your attachment to me fades, I would wander the world forever. My old existence only tortured me. I'm glad it's gone. But not completely.

You are my only tie to it. When I return to my old world, I want you in it. I so much yearn for this new world I shall soon find to give me a path to return.

LIZZY: In your last letter you say that I am the only thing in your former life that you value. You write as though you fear that my attachment to you will fade. Please believe me when I say that the tie we have to each other will only break if you break it. Your return means more to me than I can ever put on a sheet of paper.

END OF SCENE 1

Scene 2

Scene: *Henry and John are stage left in a spotlight. The rest of the stage is dark. They wear open-necked, long sleeved shirts. Periodically they wipe their foreheads with a handkerchief.*

HENRY: How long have we been here?

JOHN: Two hours.

HENRY: It seems more like two days. I still have no idea where I am. You're the artist. Look at it. What do you see?

JOHN: It looks like we've wandered into a mysteriously transported French provincial town.

> [*From off stage comes the faint sound of a brass band playing European dance music badly.*]

HENRY: With an out of tune band to match.

MUSIC RESEMBLING OFFENBACH
BEGINS TO PLAY MORE LOUDLY

> [*Lights come up on a street in Papeete, Tahiti. Both men move to down stage center and stop. Lights have come up on a scene of a public square with a bandstand. Dressed as in Gaugin's painting, Ta Matete, men in uniforms and civilian clothes and women in Tahitian and European dance.*]

MUSIC FADES

HENRY: For this, we might as well have gone back to Japan.

JOHN: Tahitian beauties, burnished like old gold. That's what those books said.

HENRY: You see before you the reason we shouldn't have taken their word for it.

JOHN: Poetic imagination strikes again. At least Lord Bryon's does.

HENRY:

> [*Somewhat sarcastically*]

> The place where nature made constitutions and lawyers unnecessary:
> The happy shores without a law,
> Where all partake the earth without dispute
> And bread itself is gathered as a fruit;

> [*MARAU enters. She wears traditional Tahitian clothing, complete with flowered lay necklace and a hibiscus bloom over one ear.*]

MARAU: Where none contest the fields, the woods, the streams:
The goldless age, where gold disturbs no dreams.

HENRY; All right, John, where am I, really? Byron quoted to us. On a Tahitian street corner.

MARAU: By a Tahitian woman in grammatically collect English. No less.

JOHN: Looking at you, it should come as no surprise that we expected a more Polynesian greeting.

MARAU: That girl's boarding school in Sydney had me memorize English poetry in hopes of wiping away all my culture.

JOHN: But they did not succeed.

MARAU: Not entirely.

HENRY: Our world has its wicked temptations.

MARAU: But tell me, where would you Americans be now if the British had monopolized all their cultural treasures?

HENRY: We'd be in a state of nature, half naked, painting ourselves red, white and blue.

MARAU: Mr. Adams, you and Mr. La Farge seem amazed that we Tahitians have moved beyond that point.

HENRY: So much for traveling the world incognito.

MARAU: Finding your name on an arriving ship's passenger list. A welcome surprise. For many reasons.

HENRY: I would be interested to know why I'm a surprise your find welcome.

MARAU: Such modesty from a writer of your renown.

HENRY: Not so much modesty as surprise that you know anything about me.

MARAU: The ships that come to Tahiti bring your books as well as you. Ones about history. And rumor has it, novels.

HENRY: As you say, rumors.

MARAU: If only your pen could talk.

JOHN: May I ask you a question?

MARAU: Of course.

JOHN: Do you need to remain incognito?

MARAU: No. You may call me Marau.

HENRY: May call. That implies there's something we may not call you.

MARAU: Your Majesty.

HENRY: Why not?

MARAU: The former king of Tahiti is also my former husband. He took that title away. When he divorced me.

HENRY: Certainly an abuse of power.

MARAU: Actually he lacks power. He's impotent in so many ways.

JOHN: I'm trying to imagine Queen Victoria saying the same thing to strangers. The image won't come.

MARAU: I have no problem saying many things Queen Victoria never would.

HENRY: I suspect that's not your only differences.

MARAU: You must also consider the similarities of royalty everywhere.

HENRY: The similarities are far from obvious.

MARAU: To make it simpler, I'll compare the two of us.

HENRY: Now you've intrigued me.

MARAU: Mr. Adams. We are both royalty.

HENRY: My presidential ancestors hearing the family name coupled with the term royalty. They would find it shocking.

MARAU: But you're not shocked, are you Mr. Adams?

HENRY: No. My family is my pride and my burden.

MARAU: I could say the same.

HENRY: Well, I've a secret to tell you that wasn't on the passenger list. I've come here to remove my past and my family's from my mind.

MARAU: No royal Tahitian would want to forget our history.

JOHN: Says the queen to the historian.

> [*Marau gives Henry a sly glance and says nothing.*]

END OF SCENE 3

Scene 4

Scene: *Adams seated in Marau's home. He sits on chair, takes a letter out of an envelope and reads it. He wears white linen trousers, has the sleeves of his white shirt rolled up to the elbows and no tie. When Marau enters, he puts the letter away and stands up.*

MARAU: Please. Sit.

> [*Henry does and so does Marau.*]

I trust your Mr. La Farge understands his exclusion. But here royal residences, unassuming as they may be, are for royals.

HENRY: Unassuming by the standards of Buckingham palace. But as I look about, poverty is not the first thing that strikes me.

MARAU: My father was a wealthy Jewish merchant.

HENRY: Now I'm thoroughly confused.

MARAU: According to Jewish law, one's mother must be a Jew for the child to be a Jew. Therefore I am a royal Teva like my mother.

HENRY: Modern day Jews and royalty of any nation are, to say the least, and unexpected mix. As I'm sure you're aware, Jews are frown upon everywhere.

MARAU: Jews wrote the Bible while your illiterate Anglo-Saxon ancestors roamed the forests half naked.

HENRY: I'll leave the Jewish part to one side. But I find it equally amazing your royal mother married a merchant.

MARAU: My father's family name was Salmon, as in Solomon, king of Israel. He was the last in a long line of Salmon ben Salmons. My mother would only marry royalty.

HENRY: You're claiming a Biblical king as your ancestor.

MARAU: King Henry VII of England claimed the mythical King Arthur as his. At least my ancestor actually lived.

HENRY: I still find it hard to believe that your mother thought of your father as royalty.

MARAU: Although the our French masters put a stop to it, in my mother's day, the child of a royal Teva and a non-royal father was strangled at birth . Yet here I am.

HENRY: I take it you realize you've just pointed out a virtue of French rule.

MARAU: They made their point. There is no need for them to stay.

HENRY: A royal revolutionary.

MARAU: As I said, our families have much in common.

HENRY: The French must be nervous. They've had more than one unhappy experience with monarch getting restored.

MARAU: The former king no long worries them. Coming from an alternative royal family, I do.

HENRY: Apparently fo good reason.

MARAU: So I hope.

HENRY: You know my great grandfather never helped raise armies. If that's what you're hoping from me, you'll be greatly disappointed.

MARAU: How do you plan to occupy your time here, Mr. Adams?

HENRY: I take it your question has something to do with the topic at hand.

MARAU: Perhaps. It will depend on your answer.

HENRY: Then to answer it, I read. Write letters.

MARAU: You're in the paradise of the world. Put down your pen. Wander, listen, observe our ways.

HENRY: I've tried.

MARAU: Perhaps not for long enough.

HENRY: The Tahitian glories I've seen are a good deal short of what Lord Byron led me to expect.

MARAU: Of course. His grandfather, not the poet, visited us.

HENRY: Surely you'll admit that playing dominos and trading toasts, in French, with your drunken ex-husband is hardly the stuff of a tropical paradise.

MARAU: King Pomare spends his life trying to be what he is not.

HENRY: I'd like to ask you something.

MARAU: Of course.

HENRY: Is that why he divorced you? Because you wouldn't play along with his fantasy of becoming a Frenchman?

MARAU: In old Tahiti divorce was a simple matter. The husband and wife just stopped living together.

HENRY: I find the whole concept of a royal divorce, any divorce, appalling. But I agree. Nothing could be simpler.

MARAU: Pomare insisted I to go before the French judge and sue him for divorce.

HENRY: Evidently gallantry is not a part of French culture he wished to absorb.

MARAU: He tried to invoke a foreign code of honor.

HENRY: How?

MARAU; He proclaimed to the court that my eldest daughter wasn't his child. Therefore he, as the injured party, was entitled to set the terms of the divorce settlement.

HENRY: I trust you had something to say after that infamous public slander.

MARAU: Why the truth, Mr. Adams. The truth. I told the court none of the children born during our marriage were his.

HENRY: I don't understand. You almost make it sound as if you glory in a dissolute sensuality.

MARAU: We make love with people who appeal to us.

HENRY: And, I take it, your husband didn't appeal to you.

MARAU: Too much alcohol and not enough honesty.

HENRY: So why did you marry him?

MARAU: My mother's family, the Tevas, represent one ancient Tahitian royal line. Pomare's upstart family another. Our families couldn't let the French divide us.

HENRY: So, a political marriage.

MARAU: Something else Queen Victoria and I have in common.

HENRY: I will tell you that I stick at the idea that married people can do whatever they desire. Royal or not.

MARAU: I can't understand why a person, royal or not, should agonize over satisfying natural desires.

HENRY: A famous British actress once said she thought it sound policy to do what you want in the bedroom as long as you don't do it in the street and frighten the horses.

MARAU: You, no doubt, have an appropriate, unflattering term for her.

HENRY: Dissolute.

MARAU: No. I would say hypocritical.

HENRY: What she tried to say in her own unfortunate way is that a line between public and private must exist.

MARA: Must is a strong word.

HENRY: You seem to have this impulse to shout out what you do.

MARAU: We live our lives naturally. Make no clever allusions. Nothing needs hiding.

HENRY: Pardon the pun, but you bare yourselves to criticism I couldn't bear.

MARAU: Criticism from whom? From our French conquerors? From visiting Americans?

HENRY: I would like to believe that there are moral standards for all humanity.

MARAU: Even if they're not the ones that make you comfortable?

HENRY: Change is usually uncomfortable.

MARAU: I take it you speak from personal experience as much as historical observation.

HENRY: In my view the historical should out weigh the personal.

MARAU: But they can't be separated. I presume like most men your age, you are married.

HENRY: I'm a widower.

MARAU: Did you always tell your late wife the truth? Did she always tell it to you?

HENRY: We wanted to spare each other's feelings.

MARAU: The truth has a way of emerging at unexpected times. In unexpected ways.

HENRY: Staying silent is a form of consideration.

MARAU: And when, inevitably, the silence is broken. What of her feelings then? And what of yours?

HENRY: All her life, we remained silent.

MARAU: And could some future historian write about your lives and the times without breaking that silence?

END OF SCENE 4

Scene 5

Scene: *Spotlight on Henry as he writes at a desk. What he writes is narrated to the audience.*

HENRY: After talking with the queen for the afternoon, we joined John in his sketching expedition. She told us we must wander over to the site of a ruined temple and see a dance. And what a dance it was.

John's eyes went wide at first, but then narrowed as he reached for his pencils. All I could do is look on in fascination. Half a dozen barefoot young women, their bodies gleaming with coconut oil, wearing only grass skirts. They moved in unison to a drum beat by chanting men. Rhythmically stamping their feet. Periodically they twirled till their skirts stood straight out.

Watching them is not like watching the performers at the Folies Bergeres. These dancers move slowly, with great dignity. Afterwards the queen told us that they were the daughters of district chiefs and this dance was their way of announcing they were now women.

> [*Lights fade on Henry. Lizzy appears at her desk, writing.*]

LIZZY: I will grant you there are unenlightened societies in which a woman who shows the hair on her head or even her face in public is considered obscene. But six bare-breasted aristocratic maidens dancing at their debutante ball? Perhaps Washington is ready for that yet.

END OF SCENE 5

Scene 6

Scene: *Henry enters their hotel room to find John working on his sketch of the Tahitian dancers.*

HENRY: When you're finished, I'd really like to buy the final painting.

JOHN: It'll be my thank you gift. No charge. But it won't become a painting until I get back to my studio.

HENRY: I'm impressed your memory keeps working even with the actual scene gone.

JOHN: Says the historian who travels to forget.

HENRY: I'm not seeking total amnesia. Some memories are worth preserving.

JOHN: I presume you have some specific ones in mind.

HENRY: I have.

JOHN: Look on my painting of the dancers when you want to keep your memories of here refreshed.

HENRY: I wonder if the woman who was once queen would sit for a portrait and become one of them.

JOHN: You could ask her.

HENRY: Better the request comes from you.

JOHN: You do stay true to form.

HENRY: I presume you have a particular form in mind.

JOHN: True to form, you're reluctant to do the asking because she's a woman and might say no.

HENRY: She has this knack of turning our conversations into unwanted explorations of my personal life.

JOHN: You're a historian and she wants to know your history. Seems appropriate. In an ironic sort of way.

HENRY: She says these cryptic things that make me think she has an agenda in mind for me.

JOHN: Since she considers you royalty, perhaps she just wants to compare notes with her own kind. Get to know you better.

HENRY: If you're right, perhaps we should think about moving on.

JOHN: I have an alternative thought for you.

HENRY: That probably involves staying here.

JOHN: It does. Become the consort of a Tahitian queen. Well, of a woman who was once a Tahitian queen.

HENRY: Very funny.

JOHN: If you ever decide to let a woman in your life again, Clover the Second would not be a good idea. No one will ever confuse the queen with Clover.

HENRY: Now which one of us can't let her memory go.

JOHN: Before we left, I told you that this trip won't do what you wanted it to do.

HENRY: I'll admit. As yet, it hasn't.

JOHN: Since we're half way around the world, that should tell you something.

HENRY: That I haven't found the right location. Why we should move on.

JOHN: Prepare. I'm going to repeat myself.

HENRY: I read somewhere that people need to hear something seven times before they learn it. Go ahead.

JOHN: You can't leave you behind.

HENRY: But it's not me I'm trying to put at a distance.

JOHN: Whoever this unnamed person is, living or dead, you need to face reality.

HENRY: I've always left fantasies, like royal marriages, to artists.

JOHN: We are literally as far away from D.C. as we can get. Any further and we head back to where we started.

HENRY: I'm not ready to do that. Yet.

JOHN: You keep using the word, yet.

HENRY: It seems appropriate.

JOHN: I think you mean never. Stop fooling yourself. When and if the queen at one remove asks you to become the Tahitian king consort...

HENRY:

[*Henry brings John to a halt.*]

Are you sure that's the proper etiquette? Does she ask me?

JOHN: She'd better. You don't even want to ask her if she'd let me paint her portrait.

HENRY: Given her attitude toward men, it may not be marriage she has in mind.

JOHN: Whatever her proposal, think very carefully before you turn her down.

END OF SCENE 6

Scene 7

Scene: *Henry and Marau are back sitting across from each other at Marau's "palace".*
Tea cups, a teapot and fruit are on the low table between them.

MARAU: Mr. Adams. You remember the last time we met, I asked your plans.

HENRY: I do. I also remember you then led our conversation off in other directions.

MARAU: Let us say I wanted to get to know you in a larger way.

HENRY: I take it you feel you've succeed.

MARAU: From the first I knew your talent for preserving the past in writing is one that I lack.

HENRY: Modesty for you. Compliments for me. And the reason is...

MARAU: I have a strong desire to make use of your talent.

HENRY: Your desire gives me a corresponding one. A strong temptation to pack up and flee.

MARAU: Flee?

HENRY: At the moment, digging into past lives doesn't suit me.

MARAU: My past. Not yours.

HENRY: Royal lives may not be identical, but they rhyme. I'd rather not.

MARAU: You run away from something besides my plan for you.

HENRY: If I say nothing on this subject, it's my polite way of encouraging you to do the same.

MARAU: Western men run from their inadequate lives or their women. You're rich, admired and can do whatever you want. So it must be a woman.

HENRY: You know your insights can become quite annoying.

MARAU: The gods wouldn't have put human beings on earth to watch them run in circles around the world and torment themselves.

HENRY: Bringing up my personal life is a form of torment.

MARAU: If you emphasize your royal side, the personal will fall away.

HENRY: I was wrong before. At least about myself. That lines doesn't exist.

MARAU: Your ancestors were presidents of your country and you are not. That doesn't mean the line no longer exists. It lies dormant. Like mine.

HENRY: Which definition of "lies" did you have in mind?

MARAU: Deflection of an uncomfortable issue. Evidence that dormant or not, your political instincts are still there.

HENRY: As you well know, American political life and Tahitian political life are miles apart in so many ways.

MARAU: Your ancestors freed themselves from an overseas power. I am looking for ways to do the same. Not so many miles apart after all.

HENRY: I'm Henry Adams. All I share with the earlier members of the Adams family is the name.

MARAU: All the more reason to join yourself to the royal Teva family. Help me write. Undermine our conquerors.

HENRY: You've said I horribly misunderstand you and your people. Why choose me?

MARAU: You taught your students about people who lived in Europe, not America.

HENRY: I did.

MARAU: Some of these people lived a thousand years ago. If I apply the same reasoning, you must have misunderstood them.

HENRY: I'm the child of those distant European people.

MARAU: By the European Bible, we could go back further. To your Adam and Eve. So do all the Tevas.

HENRY:

> [*Henry takes his index finger and draws the number one in the air and then points at Marau.*]

Touché.

MARAU: We could become the new Adams and his Eve.

HENRY: I guess that's one way for Tahiti to actually become the paradise of the world.

MARAU: When you and I unite, you become a Teva. You could write down our true heritage for the royal Tevas not yet born.

> [*Marau rises, pulls Henry to his feet. Henry looks puzzled. She puts her face against his and rubs noses with him. Then Marau kisses him on the lips. At first he seems to respond, but then he pulls away.*]

HENRY: You've already guessed. I love someone else.

MARAU: How will our uniting matter?

HENRY: I'll feel like I've betrayed her.

MARAU: Unless you join us and write our story, a whole royal line vanish from sight. And with them, a whole people.

HENRY: You tried this uniting once before. With King Pomare.

> [*Pauses, then smiles*]

Making love for a Tahitian really doesn't raise much above enjoying a good meal, does it?

MARAU: You are learning, Mr. Adams. If you do not eat life, it will eat you. But the problem remains. If the two of us do not unite, you must become a Teva in another way.

HENRY: But I haven't even agreed to help you write.

MARAU: You will. Out of boredom.

HENRY: Travel is always interesting. I won't be bored.

MARAU: If I tell the Tahitian pilots not guide any ship out of the harbor on which you are booked, your travels will end here.

HENRY: And evidently you haven't finished teaching your lesson.

MARAU:

> [*Contemplates seriously, then brightens up.*]

I shall have my mother adopt you. You shall become my brother.

HENRY: Treated like a brother. It's a role I seem destined to play.

MARAU: Well, my brother, I will speak and you will write.

HENRY: You make it sound so simple.

MARAU: It is what you have done your whole life.

HENRY: I have. But it's never simple.

> [*Marau smiles and once again rubs noses with Henry. Now, even he smiles.*]

END OF SCENE 7

Scene 8

Scene: *Henry sits at his desk in the ship. Once again, as he writes, his off stage voice says aloud what he is writing.*

HENRY: It won't be long now. Our little experiment will come to an end. I wonder. You must fret, a little impatient with me and my indecision. Do you have any idea what to do with me? If you have questions about me, you are not alone.

I hope you don't think French novels are a good model. It is possible to be as pure as an angel, yet as tormented as the wicked. I fear, my angel, I have only brought you pain. With my return, it will end. I promise with all my heart.

END OF SCENE 8

Scene 9

Scene: *Henry's living room in Washington D.C.. Clover's portrait still hangs over the mantle. Lizzy and Henry stand near each other, first looking toward the painting, and then each other.*

> *Henry throws his arms around Lizzy and gives her a long lasting kiss on the mouth. Then they sit next to each other on a sofa, holding hands.*

LIZZY: You write the most marvelous letters, but...

HENRY: I so look forward to yours, but...

[*They kiss again and break out laughing and then hug.*]

LIZZY: The Henry of old won't have done that.

HENRY: No he wouldn't.

> [*Henry hugs and kisses Lizzy again.*]

There's a way we could do that whenever we wanted.

LIZZY: And the scheme unfolds.

HENRY:

> [*Henry takes a deep breath.*]

Come away with me to the South Sea Isles.

LIZZY: You've gone from an indecisive Hamlet to becoming...

HENRY : Henry. The fifth. A-wooing.

LIZZY: And that makes me the skeptical, wooed princess.

HENRY: And are you trying to avoid answering my question?

LIZZY: Actually, I have a question for you.

HENRY: Only one?

LIZZY: It's rather all encompassing. In your letters from Tahiti you wrote about all things Tahitian. But not really about you. I really want to know what changed for you there.

HENRY: Believing that I actually can be happy.

LIZZY: I presume the attractive, divorced queen of Tahiti who kept showing up in your letters played her part in your changed outlook.

HENRY: Do I detect a hint of jealousy?

LIZZY: And do I detect more evasion.

HENRY: Marau showed me that it's possible to find happy people and join them. If I just looked, I'd find them all around.

LIZZY: I take it you did.

HENRY: We could be like them. Join them.

LIZZIE: If I came with you to the South Seas.

HENRY: Robert Louis Stevenson and Fanny live in the South Seas quite happily. I have no idea if they ever married. No one there cares.

LIZZY: Henry, do you know what living in the South Seas would be like for us?

HENRY: More than one writer has called it the paradise of the world.

LIZZY: And neither of us will be fluttering about on angel's wings. In your enthusiasm you need to keep in mind it's a very earthly paradise.

HENRY: I won't need wings to help Marau with her memoirs. Then I'll probably write a memoir of my own. Also wingless.

LIZZY: But you're a writer who spends most of his life researching in libraries. You didn't mention any Tahitian libraries in your letters.

HENRY: If I write my own memoir, I won't need them.

LIZZY: Quite the change. You writing about you.

HENRY: About how I finally became educated.

LIZZY: And then what?

HENRY: All I want to do is live out my life with you.

LIZZY: That's terribly sweet.

> [*Lizzy kisses Henry on the cheek.*]

But it won't be enough for either of us.

HENRY: Of course it will.

LIZZY: Both of us adore talking with well educated people. Let me rephrase that. People who are educated in our world.

HENRY: I'm not proposing we live on some deserted island. We'll get to know the Polynesians and their world. It'll be an adventure.

LIZZY: Other than your beautiful Tahitian queen and her family, I can't see why any non-royal Tahitian would want to know and understand us.

HENRY: Because to them we're exotic, fascinating people.

LIZZY: It would be like living among former slaves here in the South.

HENRY: I don't see the parallel.

LIZZY: Think about it. The Polynesians live like today's former slaves now live in the once-upon-a-time Confederacy

HENRY: Actually, the queen believes her memoirs will undermine the French hold on the Tahitians.

LIZZY: When it comes to the Tahitians' mentality, I'll bet even their dispossessed royalty still have the mentality of the defeated.

HENRY: When you meet Marau, you'll see she's a royal revolutionary.

LIZZY: With her book she wants to slowly dig an escape tunnel that comes out beyond the colonial walls, not blow the walls up.

HENRY: Meanwhile the Tahitians are free to follow whatever pursuit they choose.

LIZZY: As long as it's not political. Just like our black sharecroppers can pursue theirs.

HENRY: Over time...

[Lizzy cuts Henry off.]

LIZZY: It will take lots of time, if ever, for Polynesians to master their current masters. That's why the answer to your question is no.

HENRY: Then, as Marau taught me by example, I must remove my romantic robe and put on my thinker's cap.

LIZZY: A well-worn garment.

HENRY: We both know your married life isn't really a life for you.

LIZZY: You make the complicated sound so simple.

HENRY: I'd say boiled down to its essence. Not simplified.

LIZZY: No matter how hard you try, there are some things about my married life that won't boil away.

HENRY: Name them.

LIZZY: As Mrs. Senator Don Cameron, many doors open for me. Behind those doors are bright, fascinating people. Like you.

HENRY: To put a shine on your unhappiness.

LIZZY: Maybe one day divorced women...

[Henry stops her.]

HENRY: I'd never ask you to get a divorce.

LIZZY: To be together, we both know the alternative.

HENRY: We're two terribly clever people. We'll find a way to be together here, right under everyone's noses.

LIZZY: While you were away, Russian noblemen and New York financiers, with far greater resources than yours, promised to heap money on me for my favors. I turned them all down.

HENRY: I'd like to think it's because of me.

LIZZY: I'll be honest. You were far away. You said you might never come back.

HENRY: Only if you didn't want me.

LIZZIE: I do.

[*Gives Henry a kiss.*]

LIZZ: But our affair won't stay secret. And when it's discovered, I'm the one who's shunned by everyone.

HENRY: It seems you sent me around the world so that I could return to exactly where I started.

LIZZY: Henry, I sent you away so you could decide what you wanted of me. And you're back and you've decided. But it isn't what I want.

HENRY: It does seem that our roles have reversed, doesn't it

[*Lizzy shrugs her shoulders and smiles.*]

HENRY: I guess both of us received an education during my travels.

LIZZY: All we have to do now is find a way to show that education isn't in vain.

HENRY: And here I thought that women were ruled by their instincts and emotions.

END OF SCENE 9

Scene 10

Scene: *Only Henry and Lizzy's faces are visible close to each other in a single spotlight.*

HENRY: Where do you think John's paintings of the Tahitian dancers should go?

LIZZY: I'd say bare breasted maidens for your den, not the dining room.

HENRY: I meant to tell you. What I helped Marau write came up something short of Tom Pain's Common Sense.

LIZZY: Tahitian citizens were not inspired to rise up in rebellion by it.

HENRY: Marau only had enough copies of her memoir printed so that she could give them to other Tevas. Preferably royals.

LIZZY: Politics on Tahiti and politics here are many miles apart.

HENRY: I had hoped it would go beyond her. I guess I should say beyond our family.

LIZZY: Are you disappointed?

HENRY: She put on a very convincing performance as a Tahitian royal who wanted the islanders to restore her family's rule.

LIZZY: Speaking of performances, I'm really looking forward to seeing Sarah Bernhardt at Ford's.

HENRY: I've heard she does a full range of famous characters.

LIZZY: From Camille to Hamlet. But unfortunately not Henry V.

HENRY: You know Clover never found her acting convincing. Complained she's overly emotional.

LIZZY: And after all these years, do you feel we're bound to respect Clover's opinion?

HENRY: I think we should see the performance and make up our own minds.

LIZZY: Yes we should. And now, we should go. Don and the others will wonder what's happened to us.

[Spotlights pull back revealing Lizzy and Henry sitting side by side on chairs. They are dressed in 19th century formal attire. They get up.

Henry puts on a high silk hat and picks up a walking stick. Lizzy picks up a small purse. They hold hands and walk toward the doorway. Blackout]

END OF SCENE 10

Epilogue

Scene: *Henry returns to the stage, dressed as he was in the last scene.*

HENRY: A good education is a slow process. Lizzy's part in it took the rest of my life. From her I learned to cope with the unexpected. Or try to.

> [*Lizzy enters, dressed as she was in the last scene. She blows Henry a kiss and he blows one back to her.*]

LIZZY: We had a plan. Don was several years older than either of us.

HENRY: His liver couldn't last forever.

LIZZY: After he died, we'd finally get together.

HENRY: Don and you both died 1918. So did I, for that matter.

> [*Marau enters, dressed in Tahitian clothes. She goes over to Henry, throws her arms around him and kisses him full on the lips. She then laughs and stands next to Lizzy. Henry looks uncomfortable, but gathers his composure.*]

I didn't regret helping you with your memoir.

MARAU: Even though I didn't spark a revolution? Even though my father was a Jewish financier?

HENRY: Even though.

MARAU: Tell me why.

HENRY: Because you taught me that well known saying works both ways.

MARAU: Perhaps it's your sense of drama as a novelist that inspires you to leave us waiting for the saying.

HENRY: With royals of all nations, the personal is political and the political is personal. Of equal importance you taught a fellow royal that guilt and unhappiness are unneeded and personal. They have no place in politics.

When it comes to the political, even before the world I knew tore itself apart in a war, it was no longer the world I wanted. To my great regret, I lived in an age for mighty dynamos, not for virgins, holy or otherwise.

> [*Clover enters, dressed in black. She carries her camera on a tripod. She sets it down.*]

CLOVER: I'm sure everyone will notice the mention of virgins is my cue. Of greater importance, did you really think no one would notice an eleven year gap in your autobiography?

HENRY: I did write it in the last years of my life. Everyone knows old men have problems with their memory.

CLOVER: The gap does cover the time of our marriage.

HENRY: Even by the end of my life, I could never figure out how to deal with you.

CLOVER: So what did this enigma teach you?

HENRY: That love is possible even in the most unexpected circumstances.

> [*Clover motions the others to join her in front of the camera. They do. Holding a long lead for the shutter release, she counts off.*]

CLOVER: One. Two. Three!

> [*Stage lights flash and then go black.*]

END OF PLAY

THE OPTIMIST

(A Play for Radio)

CHARACTERS:

Ralph Wise
Al Green
Eleanor Burbage
Gary Pine
Vivian White
Eddie Standard
Police Officer

Scene 1

Scene: Fullbright University Garden

> [ACOUSTIC:"*We Shall Not Be Moved*".
> *Outdoor, woodland sounds like birds chirping,*
> *bees buzzing. Bottles rattle in a metal wagon.*]

AL: Don't kill it! For God's sake Ralph. Just open the jar. Then get the butterfly out of the net and stick it in gently.

> [ACOUSTIC: *Jar opens.*]

RALPH: Al, when it comes to questions of gathering and sticking, I question some of your logic.

> [ACOUSTIC: *Jar closes.*]

AL: Biology is experimental. What's the logic of a caterpillar turning into a butterfly?

RALPH: Come on. You can be logical. You just proved it.

AL: How?

RALPH: By combining one of our rare faculty union meetings with your class prep.

AL: Yeah. Here we are. Two thirds of the membership. Chasing butterflies. I did ask Eleanor, our remaining third. But, she's casting a play. Besides insects bug her.

RALPH: What I don't get is the logic of catching live butterflies when your students are just going to stick pins in them any way.

AL: Look at it this way. It's one of the few perks for a biologist teaching at Fullbright U.

RALPH: Perks?

AL: Yeah. Because we're in the middle of nowhere Indiana, I don't have to use dead insects. Like I'd have to do at Harvard or Stanford.

RALPH: No, there you'd have the money to hire a research assistant who'd spend hours catching them instead of asking me for free help.

AL: That's why on our hunt I wanted a bit of union talk. To raise my spirits.

RALPH: And exactly how could they be given a boost?

AL: By figuring out a way to get the rest of our faculty brothers and sisters to join the union. By convincing Chancellor Thatcher to spend money on people and not monuments to her ego.

RALPH: It makes sense to me, and I teach logic.

AL: The trouble is, so far our colleagues prefer genteel poverty.

RALPH: Come on, Al. Take the optimistic view.

AL: I take it the man of logic and reason can justify that statement.

RALPH: I can. It's based on that time when the union embarrassed the chancellor.

AL: What are you talking about?

RALPH: You remember don't you? Last year? Those hundred buck medical insurance over-charges we got her to refund? Didn't bunches of our colleagues congratulate us?

AL: Bunches? Did bunches of people rush up to me, shake my hand and say, "Thank you very much Al, sign me up for the faculty union."? Six people thanked me, Ralph. You don't build a union with six people out of two hundred.

RALPH: No. You start with six people.

AL: And half of those said thanks in ways that I don't find encouraging for union organizing purposes.

RALPH: How so?

AL: Let's start with Cyril. Yes, he did say "thank you". We were at neighboring uri-
nals. But before he would stand next to me, he pushed on all the stall doors
to see if anyone was there.

RALPH: I'll grant you that it's rare to find the words "academic" and "brave" used
in the same sentence but it happens, occasionally.

AL: Let's face it, Ralph, if we're hoping for collective bravery from our colleagues,
it's not goin' to happen much before those contestants in the Miss America
contest get that wish they always make for world peace.

RALPH: We need to get our colleagues' attention.

AL: You'd think big raises only goin' to the chancellor's favorites would bring
dozens and dozens of 'em into the union, would'nt you?

RALPH: We need to find something they care about even more than money.

AL: Are there enough reserved parking spaces with their names on them in the
whole world to make that happen?

RALPH: Yes!

AL: There are enough parking spaces?

RALPH: I wish, but you're on the right track.

AL: What track?

RALPH: I don't care what Karl Marx said, status matters more than money nearly
every time. What if we tied money to status?

AL: How?

RALPH: With the teachers at Oxbridge Academy. You know, that pretentious
private high school where the faculty want to send their kids, if only they
could afford it.

AL: Yeah, what about 'em?

RALPH: One of my student's applied for a job there. From what she told me, it
sounds like they'll pay her near what our place gives new humanities PhDs.

AL: Our humanities professors here qualify for food stamps and still don't join the union. What's your point?

RALPH: That is my point. When our colleagues find out they only earn as much as lowly, inferior school teachers, they'll think they've been humiliated. They'll be forced to see that logically only the union can restore their superior status.

AL: Okay, for argument's sake, let us say you're on to something. Hearsay reports from one student aren't going to convince anybody to join the union. We need more than that.

RALPH: Yes we do. We need to compare our salaries to theirs.

AL: One small problem. As employees we can get all our salaries. What about that very, very private academy?

RALPH: Where theirs are very, very confidential. I know. But what if we had a way to find out what all of them are paid?

AL: And you propose doing that by what magic?

RALPH: Having one of my ed grad students, Eddie Standard, give us their salary scale. He's the president of their teachers' union.

AL: That buttoned down air-head's president of their union?

RALPH: He is. He probably thought becoming president would increase his status. Besides, I hear no one else wanted the job.

AL: I hate to say this, Ralph, but I have a problem.

RALPH: Problem?

AL: Yes, I just graded his term paper on live butterflies' feeding habits.

RALPH: And he just did one for me on the logic of honesty. It matters because?

AL: If we ask him for confidential salary information before we hand back the papers, it'll look like we're pressuring him.

RALPH: So we'll wait until after.

AL: Then he'd think the grade's a bribe.

RALPH: You're not telling me you gave him an A on his paper, are you?

AL: No, but the paper is better than his other work in class and he got a higher grade than usual. It might look like a bribe to him and other students.

RALPH: Only if he tells any of 'em. We'll swear him to secrecy.

AL: Well doesn't that have bribe written all over it.

RALPH: Look, we need that salary comparison. It'll push the rest of our faculty toward the union. The logic's irresistible. You'll see.

AL: Maybe you're right, but my twisting Eddie's arm still seems like just a bit much.

RALPH: Okay. We'll leave you out of it. But, tell you what, let's flip for it.

AL: For what?

RALPH: Do I or don't I ask him. Here, hold my butterfly net.

> [ACOUSTIC: *Change jingles.*]

Heads I do, tails I don't.

> [ACOUSTIC: *Coin slaps on the back of Ralph's hand.*]

He's all mine.

END OF SCENE 1

Scene 2

Scene: *Ralph's Office*

[ACOUSTIC: *Brief riff on "We Shall Not be Moved." Knock on door.*]

RALPH: Come in.

[ACOUSTIC: *EDDIE walks into the office.*]

EDDIE: Have you finished my paper yet, Professor Wise? Is that why you wanted to see me? I hope nothing's wrong.

RALPH: Not that I know of, Eddie. Please, have a seat.

[ACOUSTIC: *Eddie pulls out a chair and sits.*]

I wanted to talk to you about something else, something outside of class, but here, you can have your paper back.

[ACOUSTIC: *Papers shuffled.*]

EDDIE: I got a C+? I don't know if that's right.

RALPH: Eddie, it's the best grade you've gotten so far.

EDDIE: Yeah, well any way. So why did you want to see me?

RALPH: You work at Oxbridge during the day, don't you, Eddie?

EDDIE: Yes, sir, I do and I don't mind tellin' you, I'm really proud of what I've accomplished there.

RALPH: What makes you so proud?

EDDIE: Why my students practically teach themselves.

RALPH: Teach themselves?

EDDIE: Yes, the textbook company has this website for teachers with lots and lots of questions on it. I just have a secretary pick a bunch, make copies and hand'em out to the students.

RALPH: But isn't that a lot of grading for you?

EDDIE: Oh, I let'em grade each other. They're all really smart. Everyone makes an A. It's not like here.

RALPH: I'll bet the students at Oxbridge hi have lots of advantages over the students at Fullbright.

EDDIE: What do you mean?

RALPH: I mean besides being so smart. Like coming from rich families. By the way, just how much is their tuition?

EDDIE: About thirty thousand a year.

RALPH: It's sort of like buying a new car every year, but never having a trade in.

EDDIE: I buy a new car every three years, and I have a trade in.

RALPH: So Oxbridge must pay you a pretty good salary.

EDDIE: Yeah, I'll bet it's pretty close to yours.

RALPH: Okay, consider your bet taken.

EDDIE: You'll take it? But-

RALPH: Let's see, to settle that bet the logical thing to do is compare all the salaries from official budget office figures.

EDDIE: Oh Professor Wise, I couldn't do that. Our salaries are confidential, you know.

RALPH: But you sound so proud. Wouldn't it be nice if more people knew?

EDDIE: When they see me, the way I dress, they know.

RALPH: Even so, Eddie, some of them might think maybe you weren't being completely honest about Oxbridge because you keep the salaries secret.

EDDIE: I won't try to fool them. I'm an honest person.

RALPH: I hope I can rely on that, Eddie.

EDDIE: You can, sir, but I've really gotta go now.

> [ACOUSTIC: *As Eddie exits, chair scrapes, footsteps and door closes. Immediately afterwards, knock on the door.*]

RALPH: Come in.

[ACOUSTIC: *Door opens and closes Al walks into the office.*]

AL: So? New? As our grandfathers used to say.

RALPH: Wow, you are quick.

AL: I was watching your door from the lounge. What luck?

RALPH: None, I'm afraid.

AL: You asked, directly? Not much subtlety with our mutual student.

RALPH: Directly. A bit of embarrassment on his part, that's all. He had a funny reaction to the grade on his paper, though.

AL: Funny?

RALPH: Yeah, hard to pin down. Unhappy with the grade, but couldn't bring himself to ask about it.

AL: What did you do, flunk him?

RALPH: No, he passed. Kind of like the paper he did for you. Nothing fantastic, but better than his usual.

> [ACOUSTIC: *Knock at the door.*]

Yes?

[ACOUSTIC: *Eddie opens the door and takes a few steps into the office.*]

EDDIE: Oh, hello Professor Green. I didn't expect to see you here.

AL: Hi Eddie.

EDDIE: I'm sorry to interrupt the two of you, but Professor Wise, about this paper. It's the grade you gave me. It's not really right and I can show you why.

AL: Sounds like my cue to go. I'll see you later.

[ACOUSTIC: *Al leaves and shuts the door.*]

RALPH: What's the problem with it Eddie?

EDDIE: The whole time I was walking to the elevator, the grade you gave me on the term paper, the C+. It kept bothering me.

RALPH: And what bothered you about it?

EDDIE: Well, it's hard for me to say this, but you weren't fair.

RALPH: Why's that?

EDDIE: So, since I'm so busy teaching all my classes, I use this app. It's got tons of papers on it with lots a different grades.

RALPH: I had no idea.

EDDIE: Any way, in your class I know I wasn't always there all the time. Parents' night and refereeing basketball games and all that. You know. That's why I didn't buy an A paper. I bought a B. See it's right here on my phone.

[ACOUSTIC: *More footsteps as Eddie walks to Ralph's desk.*]

EDDIE: But you gave me a C+, and that's not fair. You should raise my grade.

RALPH: Eddie, I don't know what to say.

EDDIE: Please be fair and change it to a B.

RALPH: Let me ask you this, have you ever read the Student Handbook, especially the part that talks about plagiarism?

EDDIE: Plagiarism? Isn't that another word for cheating? Are you saying I cheated?

RALPH: Let me read you what it says:

> [ACOUSTIC: *Ralph walks over to the bookcase, pulls out a pamphlet, opens it and thumbs through pages.*]

"Plagiarism is a serious offense. It is defined as using more than six words in a row that were written by someone other than the paper's author and failing to put those words in quotation marks and to identify their source."

EDDIE: But the paper I gave you had quotation marks all over it. Footnotes too.

RALPH: Here's the thing, Eddie, the Student Handbook frowns on students who do what you did.

EDDIE: I'll bet no student wrote that Student Handbook. Somebody wasn't honest.

RALPH: Here's what that same section goes on to say, "Should the course instructor deem the offense serious enough, the offender will be brought before the student court. If the court convicts the student, besides receiving a failing grade for the class, the offender will have the conviction recorded on the permanent record." So, Eddie, like it or not, those are the rules.

EDDIE: Oh Professor Wise, you're not going to turn me into the court, are you?

RALPH: The rule doesn't say I have to do it.

EDDIE: Then you'd be willing to forget it?

RALPH:No, I don't think I'd could do that either.

EDDIE: I don't understand.

RALPH: Here's what I want you to do. Write a paper using your own ideas about logic, critical thinking and honesty.

EDDIE: Oh Professor Wise, that's so unfair. I'd never criticize anyone. I just want everyone to like me.

END OF SCENE 2

Scene 3

Scene: *Costume shop back stage.*

> [ACOUSTIC: *Knock on a door, ELEANOR
> walks over to answer it and opens a rather
> creaky door.*]

ELEANOR: Brother Ralph, Brother Al, welcome to the drama department's inner sanctum.

RALPH: Sister Eleanor, we, your union siblings come bearing gifts.

ELEANOR: So Al tells me. Let me get this straight, Ralph. You blackmailed some hopelessly dense student into giving you private documents? Good job you teach logic and not ethics.

RALPH: Now, Eleanor, aren't you being a little careless with your wording?

AL: Oh, I don't know.

RALPH: I asked Eddie for the information. Once. When we first talked. He refused to give it to me. After our next discussion, quite voluntarily on his part and with no prompting from me, he produced the Oxbridge salary list and pay scale.

ELEANOR: As a bribe.

RALPH: There you go again.

AL: So what would you call it?

RALPH: I think Eddie had a chance to consider what he should do and the logic of why he should do it. After due consideration, giving us the faculty list and pay scale made sense to him.

ELEANOR: And he received nothing in return for this free gift?

RALPH: If you're implying that I didn't flunk him, you're wrong. I did.

AL: And turned him over to the student court?

RALPH: Well, under the circumstances, that seemed mean spirited.

ELEANOR: That's quite a feat of mental gymnastics you've performed there.

RALPH: So, do you wish to share my supposedly ill-gotten gains or not?

AL: You gotta be kiddin. Let's take a look.

[ACOUSTIC: *Papers are spread out on a table.*]

ELEANOR: OMG as all too many of my students say.

RALPH: Right. Look at our beginning lecturers in English with a masters.

AL: Who teach four, thirty student classes a semester and get $35,000 a year.

ELEANOR: And $55,000 for the beginning English teachers with masters at Oxbridge.

RALPH: With fewer students. Modesty prevents me from breaking into a victory dance.

ELEANOR: Seems like all we have to do is write this up, get it to the faculty and prepare for the rush.

RALPH: Once we get the information out, people a lot less bright than our colleagues would see the logic of joining a union.

AL: Aren't we missing a step?

ELEANOR: What step?

AL: How do we get the information to them?

RALPH: Email?

AL: Who reads their email?

ELEANOR: A note slipped under their office door?

RALPH: Some of our colleagues haven't been to their offices in years. They're afraid some student might find them there and ask a question they can't answer.

AL: What about their mailboxes in the department office?

ELEANOR: We could put the flyers in those red-bordered envelopes like the administration uses for official memos.

RALPH: Sounds like a sensible plan. Eleanor, why don't you call that local printer, you use for theater programs? I'll deal with the mailroom bureaucrats. No point in doing all this work if we're the only ones who see it.

END OF SCENE 3

Scene 4

Scene: *Eleanor on the telephone.*

> [ACOUSTIC: *Beeps as Eleanor dials her cell phone.*]

ELEANOR: Mr. Arbuckle? Eleanor Burbage here. [*pause*] Just fine. Look I've got a project for you. [*pause*] No, not programs. Union flyers. [*longer pause*] Mr. Arbuckle, Mr. Arbuckle. [*pause*] No, I'm not a communist. I don't think the party even exists in the U.S. any more. [*pause*] Have I ever been a communist? I'm not sure I understand what that has to do with printing the flyers. [*pause*] You're welcome to tell Chancellor Thatcher anything you like, but are you willing to print the flyers? [*pause*] Isn't that double what you usually charge?

END OF SCENE 4

Scene 5

Scene: *Ralph on the telephone.*

> [ACOUSTIC: *Beeps as Ralph dials his cell phone.*]

RALPH: Hello, Mr. Bobbit? This is Professor Wise from the philosophy department. About those flyers I brought down to the mailroom. [*pause*] Yes, I filled out all the forms there. If yours somehow got misplaced, I kept a copy of each one. [*pause*] What was in the flyers? Why do you need to know? [*pause*] Yes, I know that distribution of libelous material is illegal. [*pause*] So, after you phoned, what did Chancellor Thatcher's office have to say?

> [ACOUSTIC: *Sound of a heavy duty shredding machine. "We Shall Not be Moved".*]

END OF SCENE 5

Scene 6

Scene: *Ralph's office.*

ELEANOR AND AL: We're here.

RALPH: Come on in. Why don't you close the door and have a seat. You two are going to need to hear this sitting down.

> [ACOUSTIC: *Door closes, footsteps across the office, chairs pulled out.*]

The chancellor ordered the people in the mailroom to shred all our flyers.

AL: And did our least favorite chancellor give a reason for violating our free speech rights?

RALPH: Said they were libelous and that she was only saving us from prosecution.

ELEANOR: I'll grant you this, Ralph. It sure looks like Madame T's genuinely scared of what we're doing. So what? We have to do them all over again?

RALPH: I've got an idea. One of my former students managed to hang onto her job at the local newspaper after downsizing. We still talk. Maybe I can convince her to do a summary of what we've found. If we're lucky, she'll put it next to the obituary page.

AL: Why there?

RALPH: I hear a lot of the over-the-hill faculty read it regularly to see if their death notices appear prematurely. My sources tell me the chancellor sends in fake notices as a sign of her disfavor.

ELEANOR: Our colleagues headed for the nursing home may not be our best pool for potential union members.

RALPH: To win union recognition, we'll need every vote we can get.

ELEANOR: So?

RALPH: So, besides the newspapers, like you said, we should stick to the plan. Let's do the whole thing all over again. This time, handwritten envelopes. Caesar Chavez stamps on them, if they exitist. We'll mail the flyers to everyone's home address. A bit old-fashioned, but they'll know it's not junk mail.

AL: Let me ask you something else. How much money do we have in our treasury after paying for the shredded flyers?

RALPH: As treasurer of our union local I can say without fear of contradiction that the last time I looked we had about a buck and a quarter.

ELEANOR: The bank is unlikely to give us a loan for the difference.

RALPH: Don't worry. Once all those cards and union dues start rolling in, I'll have the pleasure of presenting the treasurer with a bill and get paid in full.

[ACOUSTIC: *Riff on "We Shall Not be Moved".*]

END OF SCENE 6

Scene 7

Scene: *Faculty lounge.*

[ACOUSTIC: *Paper crinkling, tea pot whistling, coffee maker making noises.*]

AL: How many cards have come back?

RALPH: After today's mail, containing one single card, we're up to eight. More than twice our original membership.

AL: We should try to get your former student to announce the results of our recruiting drive in the newspaper that way.

RALPH: My devious ways are rubbing off on you.

AL: Only five new members! If I had any sense, I'd give up.

RALPH: I really thought we were on to something with this. I really did. I can't figure out what happened. The logic seemed so overwhelming.

[ACOUSTIC: *GARY'S footsteps sound as he walks across the lounge.*]

GARY: Greetings and salutations to one and all.

AL: Hi Gary. And on your happy, optimistic greeting, I'll head back to my lab and promise not to be too mean to my students.

[ACOUSTIC: *Al walks out.*]

GARY: And what was that all about?

RALPH: Both of us 've had something of a hard time of late. Logically speaking there must be a way out, if I could think of it.

GARY: I like a man who uses his academic discipline to bring order to his life.

RALPH: I have a starting point for this problem solving in mind. Years ago I use to keep a bottle of scotch in my office. Maybe it's time to see if I can find it. Care to join me?

GARY: I would indeed. Rest assured, if yours has vanished, you can always rely on mine.

RALPH: Before we start our treasure hunt, would you mind telling me something?

GARY: The living reincarnation of Henry VIII stands at your service.

RALPH: I had something more modern in mind than your alter-ego, if that's possible.

GARY: King Henry and I seldom part company, but you have our permission to ask what you will.

RALPH: Okay, you got the flyer and the union card, didn't you?

GARY: Yes, indeed.

RALPH: And did you read the flyer before you threw it out?

GARY: With great interest and also that article in the newspaper next to the obituaries. So did most of the members of my department. Lots of chatter.

RALPH: And did you think we made the case that the professors at our institution of higher learning are losing ground to those teachers at the local snob-school?

GARY: Rafe, my good man, you made it very well. Your graphs and charts were easy to read and your prose a model of clarity. For your gifted writing, Henry VIII would have appointed you to his privy council.

RALPH: Then tell me, did the stuff about the salaries make you angry even a little bit?

GARY: Angry? Furious! How could Chancellor Thatcher allow a pretentious high school to pay better salaries than ours? It's outrageous, an unconscionable slight. It shows no respect for the natural order of the world. Everybody said so.

RALPH: But as outraged as all of you are, you still didn't join the union. Would you please tell me why?

GARY: Many of us did talk about the situation. But, in the end, we all felt those fly-ers humiliated the whole faculty. And then that newspaper article announced our lowly status to the world. After that, how could we ever trust you and your organization not to embarrass us again?

[ACOUSTIC: *"We Shall Not Be Moved"*]

END OF SCENE 7

Scene 8

Scene: *Ralph's Office.*

> [ACOUSTIC: *Knock at the door, the door opens.*]

RALPH: Eleanor, Al, hi, glad you could make it on such short notice. Come in.

> [ACOUSTIC: *Two sets of footsteps, chairs pulled out.*]

ELEANOR: So what's the big emergency? Let me guess. You've had another perfectly logical idea you're sure will have the faculty joining the union in droves.

RALPH: All right, have your fun. One of these days I'm going to figure out a logical way so that droves of 'em will join.

AL: So why are we here?

RALPH: You remember how way back when the three of us volunteered for the faculty senate events committee?

ELEANOR: Vaguely. Wanted to prove what a waste of time all these committees were.

RALPH: Right. Because unless the chancellor gave us a budget, there was no point planning events. As I recall, I even said I'd act as chair of the non-functioning committee.

AL: Yeah, so?

RALPH: Well, as chair I get this phone call, from the chancellor's office. Suddenly we have money.

ELEANOR: I'm suspicious already.

RALPH: As well you should be.

AL: Because?

RALPH: Her eminence dumped all this money on the events committee because she wants us to organize a popular campus lecture series.

ELEANOR: Popular? What does she mean by popular?

RALPH: For the press and public, especially T.V. And she wants it yesterday.

AL: Or what? She will cut our non-existent pay raises in half? Speaking of which, what do these faculty get for this faculty lecture series? Money? Time off?

RALPH: Her sincerest thanks. By the way, we have permission to use her name. In fact she insists on it. The Chancellor Thatcher Invitational Lecture Series. Not quite having her name on a building, but close enough.

ELEANOR: So we're supposed to choose the lambs to be sacrificed on the alter of the chancellor's ego. That should make us popular with our colleagues.

RALPH: It gets better. She only wants us to pick the lambs who've national or, better yet, international reputations.

AL: Great. Talk about a no-win situation. The ones we pick'll hate us for the extra work, and everyone else'll hate us because we think they're nobodies.

RALPH: Why do you think she's asked us to pick the faculty?

ELEANOR: Would I be wrong in thinking that as a perfectly logical human being, you have already devised a plan?

RALPH: You would not. So here's my idea. Rather than tryin' to talk a half a dozen unfortunate souls into this, we could pick just one and see how it goes.

ELEANOR: Well done, Ralph. What if the first lecture is a disaster? What if the chancellor decides she doesn't want any more? Then we don't have to un-invite the five angry people.

RALPH: Okay, it's agreed, just one egotistical fool will be sent to the top of the flag pole for saluting purposes. Al, you've got a few people in science who'd fit the bill, don't you? What about Angus?

AL: The man who's thought of thirty-six ways of putting arsenic in the food chain? Every would-be spouse poisoner in town'll show up. Do you really want to send him out in front of T.V. cameras? Eleanor, what about Osric?

ELEANOR: The self-professed world's greatest actor who always manages to feel up his leading ladies? The #MeToo audience for that should be fun too.

RALPH: Which leaves us with what?

ELEANOR: Gary, the world's greatest expert on Henry VIII. Since both of you became single men, a drinking buddy of yours, or so I've been told. You can ask him.

RALPH: A few beers at the bowling alley and a bit of tale swapping, that's all. Look, he needs an audience. I need to be reminded that someone else besides me can make a fool of himself with women.

ELEANOR: Gary's what? Divorced now for the fourth time? None beheaded. Not quite Henry, but close, close enough.

RALPH: You exaggerate. It's only his third divorce.

AL: I miss all the good gossip buried in a laboratory. But he sounds great, just what we're after.

RALPH: Eleanor, I suppose proposing Gary has nothing to do with that new woman in English on your Women's Studies Committee, the one who does Henry's Ann Boleyn?

ELEANOR: You have my word on it, Boy Scouts honor. They're coed now, you know.

RALPH: Right, I know a set-up when I see one. She'll come and make Gary wish he hadn't wanted to.

ELEANOR: All right, I'll admit it. Vivian could use a bit of media attention for her tenure file. And everybody's heard of Gary and Henry VIII.

RALPH: Henry meeting Ann, it didn't turn out so well.

ELEANOR: Come on, these two flakes are made for each other. We're just providing the audience. Do you want a formal motion?

RALPH: No, it's all right. I know when I'm out-numbered.

AL: One final motion, then. That the chair of this committee should be charged with the task of convincing Professor Gary Pine to give the very first talk in the Chancellor Thatcher Invitational Lecture Series. And if he fails, he shall be forced to serve another term as committee chair.

ELEANOR& AL: Aye.

RALPH: No!

ELEANOR: Sorry Ralph, the ayes have it.

END OF SCENE 8

Scene 9

Scene: *Bar in the local bowling alley.*

> [ACOUSTIC: *Riff on "Greensleeves". Noise of a bowling alley: talking, pins falling, balls rolling, glasses clinking.*]

GARY: The king grants you our permission to rise. When participating in sporting activities with royalty, it is not necessary to maintain a subservient position.

RALPH: Just tying a shoelace to keep from breaking my neck. But I appreciate your consideration.

GARY: There will be no necks broken or severed except by my explicit command so, Rafe my good man, do finish. You've been lucky. Are you now ready for the drubbing you have so far avoided?

RALPH: I've had my fill. So as a consolation prize for your missed opportunity, and as a reward for bowling 300, the next round of drinks is on me.

GARY: That's awfully generous of you since it took me all three games to get that 300.

RALPH: 300 is such an impressive number in bowling. Whether it takes you one line or three, is beside the point.

GARY: If I still wore that ruby ring, I'd let you kiss it as a token of my appreciation. But my last wife got it in lieu of the good steak knives.

RALPH: I had no idea Henry VIII could be bought so easily.

GARY: He probably couldn't, but his twenty-first century version lacks his financial resources.

RALPH: I'm sorry to hear it.

GARY: There are, of course, some non-material things we value beyond all others.

RALPH: Such as?

GARY: I'll tell you this. The original Henry's wives are not among them. Did you hear that the Woman's Studies Committee actually has some new woman on it with nice things to say about Ann Boleyn?

RALPH: Well, as I recall, Henry had some nice things to say about Ann, at least until the very end.

GARY: When he had her head cut off.

> [ACOUSTIC: *Loud sound of bowling ball striking pins.*]

I consider that his final verdict on her and therefore mine.

RALPH: Do you know, I think I've got a scheme that would give you a chance to have your crack at her. Maybe even find an audience for your clash.

GARY: Oh, really?

RALPH: My confidential sources tell me that the chancellor's planning to sponsor a public lecture series on campus. Newspapers, T.V. invited, the full treatment. As chair of the events committee, I could propose your name to her as the first speaker.

GARY: Do you think she'd agree to that? All those scientists always pester her for attention.

RALPH: I think I can talk her and the committee 'round into having you kick off the series and saving the pesky scientists until later.

GARY: What about this Ann Boleyn woman? How do we know she'll make an appearance?

RALPH: I'll tell you what. I'll stop by her office and extend a personal invitation.

GARY: And coming from a senior colleague, personally darkening her door, she could hardly turn you down, could she? Not quite a royal command, but close, very close. Well, this should be fun.

RALPH: And what are you going to call the talk?

GARY: "Henry VIII: Ruler of His Own Destiny."

> [ACOUSTIC: *Sound of ball knocking down bowling pins, loudly.*]

END OF SCENE 9

Scene 10

Scene: *VIVIAN's office.*

> [ACOUSTIC: *"Greensleeves" played briefly.*]

RALPH: Knock, knock.

VIVIAN: Let's see, I'm supposed to say, "Who's there?" Then you're supposed to say what?

RALPH: The man with an offer I hope you won't refuse.

VIVIAN: Somehow, I don't think that's a good poetic choice for the next line.

RALPH: Why? Just because not much rhymes with refuse?

VIVIAN: I can only say, pray excuse, and then think of what you will lose.

RALPH: All right, you win. So let me just introduce myself. I'm Ralph Wise from the philosophy department. I try to make sense out of things.

VIVIAN: How appropriate. A man named Wise in search of wisdom.

RALPH: Well, not exactly. When my lot came over to the U.S. a few generations ago, the family's name was Weiss. Some Ellis Island clerk who wasn't up on his Yiddish wrote down Wise.

VIVIAN: What an amusing coincidence. About a century ago some Ellis Island clerk who was up on his Yiddish turned my great grandfather's name from Weiss to White. Of course coming on a jet plane to JFK from Ethiopia by way of Tel Aiv, my mother didn't have to worry about a new identity.

RALPH: Ah, my mother should finally be happy. I've met a nice Jewish girl. Though maybe not the one she was expecting.

VIVIAN: As long as we're playing the coincidence game, let me try one more. Harry Houdini.

RALPH: Good old Eric Weiss! The family story is that he was my great-grandfather's cousin.

VIVIAN: I guess that makes us kissing cousins.

RALPH: If I'd said that, some people would call it sexual harassment. And then I couldn't in good conscience make the proposition I came to make.

VIVIAN: Sorry, I didn't mean to be so forward. It's just that I'm kind of lost right now with Ann Boleyn and her unhappy kissing cousin, Thomas Wyatt.

RALPH: Unhappy kissing cousin?

VIVIAN: Well, what do you make of this by Wyatt:
"They flee from me that one time did me seek
With naked foot stalking in my chamber."
Doesn't it sound like a man who had everything he wanted? Then along came King Henry. But I don't know.

RALPH: Sounds like enough for most of the lit people I know. Which brings me back again to why I stopped by.

VIVIAN: But I need more than that. To be really, really sure, I've got to play it out as close to the original as I can get it.

RALPH: After your kissing cousins crack, that sounds like a pick-up line if I've ever heard one. As appealing as that is, I'd like to leave it to one side for now and get back to why I'm here.

VIVIAN: Just when I thought that my research and my life were coming together.

RALPH: Let me see if at long last I can offer you a prospect that is at least as appealing as a distant cousin, something that could help bring your life and research in line.

VIVIAN: Which would be?

RALPH: The real reason I stopped by. I'd heard about you and your research. And I'd guessed you'd heard of Gary Pine.

VIVIAN: Heard of him? Why do you think I took the job here?

RALPH: To unify your life and your research?

VIVIAN: There you have it. I've really, really looked forward to finding a modern day Henry.

RALPH: Really, really? Well, then what good luck I stopped by. Gary's going to be giving a public lecture about Henry VIII on the first Friday of next month. A committee I'm on set it all up. We'd hoped we could talk you into putting in an appearance.

VIVIAN: King Henry would have to imprison me to keep me away.

RALPH: As I recall, that didn't happen until much later in their relationship.

VIVIAN: Let's see if our modern day Henry can figure that out.

[ACOUSTIC: *"Greensleeves" riff*]

END OF SCENE 10

Scene 11

Scene: *Lecture hall at the university.*

GARY: So, let me bring this talk to an end by restating my premise. Henry made the decisions. Everyone else reacted. No one forced him or beguiled him into marrying any of his wives. He ruled his own destiny.

[ACOUSTIC: *Strong applause.*]

RALPH: Thank you so much Professor Pine for that insightful and entertaining talk. Would you be willing to take questions from the audience?

GARY: I look forward to answering them.

RALPH: Professor White has a question for you.

VIVIAN: Actually, I have an alternative explanation. Witchcraft. Ann beguiled him.

[ACOUSTIC: *Low level tittering in the audience.*]

GARY: Let me guess. You must either be a member of the Women's Studies Committee or the local coven.

[ACOUSTIC: *Snickering from the audience.*]

VIVIAN: Now Professor Pine, there's more than one way to look at the world. Even Shakespeare thought witches were better at it than most humans.

[ACOUSTIC: *Scattered applause.*]

GARY: And tell me, Professor White, what could witchcraft possibly add to our understanding of Henry's relationship with Ann?

VIVIAN: Ann used witchcraft to ensnare Henry. She wasn't beautiful and she certainly wasn't royal. Henry had no reason to pay attention to Ann for more than a moment or two. But he did. He behaved like a man bewitched.

GARY: It was his free will choice. He tried a royal princess, and she failed him. He needed someone he could control.

VIVIAN: But he couldn't control her. She controlled him, won him over with charm. She'd studied him, observed him. She knew how to arouse him. More importantly, she knew when and how to refuse him. No, by today's standards charm is too mild a word. [Singing] It's witchcraft, strictly taboo.

> [ACOUSTIC: *Laughter then sustained applause.*]

GARY: I didn't come here to have someone with no genuine historical knowledge treat me and a life-time of research like a joke. Your statements are outrageous.

WOMEN FROM AUDIENCE: You are a joke, you chauvinist pig!

MAN FROM AUDIENCE: Why don't you keep your mouth shut, you feminazi!

> [ACOUSTIC: *Uproar from the audience.*]

RALPH: Perhaps this is a good point to thank everyone for coming, especially our friends the local media, and to bring our discussion to a close.

> [ACOUSTIC: *Continued general yelling and shouting, chairs shoved, people exiting until the last echoes of the audience fade.*]

GARY: That's just what I'd expect from some fan of Ann Boleyn.

RALPH: A fan? Like you're a fan of Henry VIII? Both of you are so tuned to these people that the line between you and them has gotten all fuzzed up. You'd better find a way to lock them up in your desk drawers at night, or someone will have you two locked up.

GARY: I'm not done with her.

RALPH: You're not listing, are you? Look, I don't think Madam Chancellor will go for another lecture on Henry, or Ann, for that matter.

GARY: No, the next chat between the two of us needs to be a much more intimate affair.

RALPH: Intimate? You're really nuts, aren't you? If you've got this need to talk with her some more, stop by her office. Email her.

GARY: I'm not going on to her turf and I'm not making the first approach. That gives her the advantage.

RALPH: Make it sound informal. Ask her out to lunch.

GARY: That sounds like I'm begging. You've got to arrange something.

RALPH: Me?

GARY: Yes, you. You were the one who got me into this mess. Now you can make a contribution toward giving me the final say, the very last word. It befits a king.

RALPH: Come on. You've got to be kidding. Arrange an intimate meeting between someone who thinks he's Henry VIII with someone who thinks she's Ann Boleyn?

GARY: Face it, it's a little late now to worry about Henry and Ann getting together again, isn't it? You already arranged that, haven't you?

RALPH: And now, figuratively speaking, there's blood all over the floor. You want more?

GARY: You've got to help me take this first bloody meeting with her to its logical conclusion. You're the one who's always saying logic and reason are what count.

RALPH: Yes, I do, but what you're asking isn't logical or reasonable.

GARY: You have to call her. Make that call and, and I'll join your union.

RALPH: You're that desperate?

GARY: Do it and I'll remember you for all eternity.

RALPH: Okay, okay, I'll take care of it.

[ACOUSTIC: *Phone beeps as Ralph dials.*]

RALPH: Hello, Vivian. This is Ralph. Glad I caught you. Do you bowl by any chance?

END SCENE 11

Scene 12

Scene: *Bowling Alley.*

> [ACOUSTIC: *Bowling alley sounds.*]

RALPH: Okay, as your referee and chaperone, I'm calling a halt to this fight. You know the rules. You need to go to your neutral corner after a knock down.

GARY: Relax, Ralph, no blood, no foul. We're just having a good time.

VIVIAN: Does rolling a bowling ball count as a retreat to a neutral corner? Because if it does, then Cousin Ralph, you're the one who needs to go to it.

RALPH: Your wish is my command.

> [ACOUSTIC: *Sound of Ralph's footsteps. After a pause, bowling ball rolls down the alley, pins go down.*]

VIVIAN: I 've got to tell you. Even though we won't ever see Henry and Ann the same way, I really, really admire the way you make Henry part of you. Like you can see the world the way he saw it.

GARY: That's very kind of you. You know some of my colleagues see my enthusiasm as an act. You're one of the few people I've run into who realize that it's more than that for me.

VIVIAN: You're no phony, you're not. I can tell.

> [ACOUSTIC: *More sound of pins going down and Ralph returning.*]

RALPH: All right, Gary, the pins didn't react to finesse. Maybe they'll respect your brute force.

GARY: Prepare yourselves for a demonstration of one of Henry's many talents.

> [ACOUSTIC: *Gary walks off. Bowling ball rolls, pins go down.*]

VIVIAN: I see there are limits to Wyatt's accomplishments.

RALPH: Vivian, I don't know how to break this to you, but Wyatt never went into a bowling alley.

VIVIAN: Your performance this evening is proof enough of that. If he had, I'm sure you would've done better.

RALPH: From what I read, he's interesting. But that doesn't mean I want to become him.

VIVIAN: But, you're my sweet cuz. If you don't become him, how will I ever truly understand the world the way he sees it? Look at how Gary absorbs Henry. He's a really, really fine model for you.

RALPH: Look, as you can tell from the lecture, lots of people think that model's a joke.

VIVIAN: Including you?

RALPH: Let's just say I have found him amusing, at times.

VIVIAN: Don't you see? It takes courage to merge with the past, to get so far inside someone that all the boundaries vanish. Then their accomplishments become your accomplishments.

RALPH: I don't understand the logic of that. Isn't it kind of like you're plagiarizing someone's lifetime achievements?

VIVIAN: Ralph, you'll see. Up close works much better than far away. If you don't merge your life with theirs, if you don't let them merge with you, you'll always miss the best part.

> [ACOUSTIC: *Sound of pins falling. Gary walks back.*]

GARY: There! Royal honor upheld. Beat that, milady, if you can.

[ACOUSTIC: *Vivian walks away.*]

RALPH: Think this could be your night?

GARY: My points about Henry had her on the ropes.

RALPH: I was talking about the bowling, Gary.

GARY: True, True. She'll need three strikes in the tenth frame to beat my score.

[ACOUSTIC: *Sound of pins falling.*]

That's only one.

[ACOUSTIC: *Sound of pins falling.*]

RALPH: And that's two.

[ACOUSTIC: *Short riff on "Greensleeves".*]

END OF SCENE 12

Scene 13

Scene: *Eleanor's prop room.*

> [ACOUSTIC: *Hangers moved on metal coat rack.*]

ELEANOR: These costumes are a mess. Sorry. You were saying?

RALPH: You've done a nice job of staying out of sight since the big event.

ELEANOR: Sorry, sorry. Pre-occupied with finding believable props. A believable cast would be nice too. Are you feeling abandoned? What about the chancellor?

RALPH: Without giving you a verbatim transcript, let's just say we're off the hook for finding more speakers.

ELEANOR: Well done Ralph!

RALPH: Like I keep saying, some times logic and optimism work hand in hand. My guess is she's looking for something a bit less unintentionally amusing and a whole lot less confrontational.

ELEANOR: Yeah, that picture of Gary drawing his finger across his throat with the caption "Modern day Henry VIII expresses his opinion of a colleague" is all over the web.

RALPH: Her Eminence did send me a thank-you note for organizing what she now calls the faculty lecture series. Signed herself Chancellor Thatcher, F.U.

ELEANOR: My, my.

RALPH: Perhaps she was just too busy to write out Fullbright University. So what's up with you?

ELEANOR: Well, I'm trying to sort out the cast for *Much Ado About Nothing* for the civic in town.

RALPH: Problems?

ELEANOR: Always problems in town. Here on campus when I cast a play, I just point to students – You! You! and You! Show up tomorrow.

RALPH: Gee, I guess Gary's right. Monarchy isn't dead.

ELEANOR: In town it sure is. I have to hold my breath with every production and hope the talent appears, or beg somebody to take a role with my fingers crossed. I hate it when people laugh in my face.

RALPH: Why don't you do *Ann of a Thousand Days* instead?

ELEANOR: And how does that solve my casting problems?

RALPH: I've got your Henry and your Ann. Boy do I have 'em. I have them at lunch. I have them at dinner. I have them every time I turn around.

ELEANOR: You mean their encounter wasn't just a one time thing?

RALPH: If the word, inseparable, ever had any meaning, it means the two of them.

ELEANOR: Do I detect just a hint of resentment in your voice? Relax, you'll find other drinking buddies, or is something else going on here?

RALPH: Like what?

ELEANOR: Like you saw her first.

RALPH: Busted.

ELEANOR: So tell me, after that stunner of a Naomi Campbell look-alike you married the first time around, why Vivian?

RALPH: Wit has its attractions. And speaking of look-alikes, you know what? I found Ann Boleyn's picture on the web. From the right angle, skin tones aside, Vivian looks like her.

ELEANOR: Well there's an interesting coincidence.

RALPH: Coincidence? It scared the crap out of me. If I remember my undergraduate history right, once Henry and Ann met, nothing else seemed to matter to them. And to put it mildly, it didn't lead either of 'em to their best moments.

ELEANOR: It's a free world and they're both adults.

RALPH: Says who? Have you ever had one of those dreams where you see two people near a cliff? You keep shouting at them to watch out, but they don't hear you? Well, all of a sudden that dream is my life.

ELEANOR: Why Ralph, I didn't know you cared so deeply about preventing human folly.

RALPH: A truly great actress would have sounded a good deal less sarcastic.

ELEANOR: This discussion isn't about me, Ralph.

RALPH: Okay, I've admitted it. I think Vivian's interesting. Yes, I know. It's not logical or sensible. It's just that I've never run into anyone quite like her before. But things being what they are between her and Gary, that's beside the point.

ELEANOR: And what is the point?

RALPH: At first it seemed so logical. Have her chat with Henry, er Gary. You know, sort of like having two people in an insane asylum who both think they're Napoleon meet at lunch. It only makes sense that a sharp dose of reality will restore logical thinking.

ELEANOR: And how was logical thinking supposed to help you this time?

RALPH: It was supposed to discredit my competition. Well, it didn't work. What's worse, with this pair, putting the two of them together made 'em wackier. It feels like my fault that two screwed up people are getting even more screwed up.

ELEANOR: Where is the optimistic man we've all come to know?

RALPH: Trying as hard as he can to make sense of it all.

[ACOUSTIC: *"Greensleeves"* riff.]

END OF SCENE 13

Scene 14

Scene: *Ralph's office.*

VIVIAN: Sweet cuz, shouldn't leave your door open. Anyone might walk in.

RALPH: No one will ever confuse you with just anyone, but do come in.

> [ACOUSTIC: *Vivian walks across the office, pulls out a chair and sits.*]

VIVIAN: It's all your fault, you know. Everything that's happened. And I don't know how Gary and I can ever thank you.

RALPH: Somehow or other, you'll find a way. So what's up?

VIVIAN: We were going to tell you together, but you know Gary's away giving a paper, so I talked him into letting me do it. You should be the first to know. The world is about to come full circle for us.

RALPH: The British parliament has deposed the current royal family and installed Gary and you as king and queen?

VIVIAN: That comes next, but first we're getting married.

> [ACOUSTIC: *"Greensleeves played softly under the rest of the scene.*]

RALPH: I'm trying to think of the appropriate words, but somehow or other they just won't come out.

VIVIAN: That's okay, sweet cuz. When Ann told Wyatt about marrying Henry, I'm sure he said the same thing to her, or something very like it.

RALPH: I'll take your word for it. I've got no reason to disbelieve someone who was there, at least in spirit.

VIVIAN: There's one more thing that Gary and I would like you to consider, and please don't say no.

RALPH: Which is?

VIVIAN: Would you be our best man?

RALPH: I could be clever and ask what Wyatt did.

VIVIAN: He went away, and wrote poetry.

RALPH: A wise man.

VIVIAN: I know you're uneasy about us, but please say you will. I'll always remember you for this.

RALPH: Funny, Gary used almost those exact same words when he asked me to arrange for the two of you to meet at the bowling alley.

VIVIAN: You see, despite Gary's and my differences, we do think alike.

RALPH: I've noticed.

VIVIAN: Be happy Ralph. I care about you. I really, really want to see you happy. I'd do anything to make you happy.

RALPH: Anything covers a lot of territory

VIVIAN: Yes it does, my sweet cuz, yes it does.

END OF SCENE 14

Scene 15

Scene: *The living room of Gary's house.*

[ACOUSTIC: *Sounds of clean-up after a meal.*]

GARY: Rafe, my good, good man, let me tell you, it was a king-sized surprise. I didn't think the venison stew would go over, but there's hardly anything left. Our colleagues are more cosmopolitan than I thought.

VIVIAN: We hadn't planned on doing the wedding feast this way, sweet cuz.

GARY: Then my last ex hit a deer a couple of weeks back. This state trooper said she could have half the carcass. She was kind enough to offer part of her share to us.

RALPH: The part that got hit by the car. Road kill doesn't seem like the image you'd wanted for the modern version of a sixteenth century marriage that had its share of problems.

GARY: Lack of boy children, that's what messed them up. I've never had kids, don't want kids of any description. We'll make up for our earlier royal counter-parts. After five centuries, we'll get it right. Even if they didn't.

RALPH: The whole world will be watching. At least most of the campus will.

GARY: Royalty never shies away from center stage. But I think it's time I made a graceful exit from this stage. Sweetheart, why don't you say a brief final good night to our best man and join me upstairs?

RALPH: I admire your enthusiasm.

VIVIAN: But first, shall we tell him?

GARY: Ralph can keep a secret. I think we can.

VIVIAN: We decided to be true to the intentions but not the deeds of our former selves. They wanted to wait until marriage before they had, as they said in Tudor England, carnal knowledge of each other. In the end they couldn't quite hold out. We've waited.

RALPH: Wait no longer.

[ACOUSTIC: *Gary crosses the room.*]

VIVIAN: So, sweet cuz, do you really wish us well?

RALPH: I certainly wish you a better fate than your sixteenth century counterparts. You especially.

VIVIAN: I really, really believe that now I'm on my way to all I've ever wanted. And my sweet, sweet cuz, be optimistic. I have much in store that will really, really please you too.

[ACOUSTIC: *"Greensleeves"*]

END OF SCENE 15

Scene 16

Scene: *Gary and Vivian's bedroom.*

[ACOUSTIC: *Vivian giggles.*]

GARY: I don't know. I think when your camera flashed, it put me off. You really took me by surprise.

VIVIAN: Just wanted a remembrance of you in all your glory, but perhaps I should have waited a bit before I immortalized you. Maybe the next time you'll be able to rise to the occasion.

GARY: Look, I'm not exactly a novice at this. There's more than one way to please you, isn't there?

VIVIAN: Of course there is, your Highness. Perhaps when you get back.

[ACOUSTIC: *Jet plane taking off*]

Are you pleased?

RALPH: Of course, but confused too.

VIVIAN: Why so, sweet cuz?

RALPH: If you wanted me, why marry Gary?

VIVIAN: Some times you really, really puzzle me. Did Ann marry Wyatt? Of course she didn't.

RALPH: So, then, what? Just a bit of adultery for your version of her modern day equivalent?

VIVIAN: I can't help being Ann. Besides, I'm entitled. Even more than Ann, with all her problems, I'm entitled.

[ACOUSTIC: *Jet plane landing.*]

GARY: That's the problem. It's all this traveling, the jet lag. It throws me off. Do you know what time it is in Auckland? Henry never had to deal with that.

VIVIAN: Perhaps after your next trip, sweetheart. I'm willing to wait for as long as it takes.

[ACOUSTIC: *Jet plane taking off.*]

RALPH: Has it ever occurred to you that one night he could come home unexpectedly from London or Sydney or wherever?

VIVIAN: That's where Houdini comes in.

RALPH: Houdini?

VIVIAN: If it happens, our cousin will protect us. We'll both escape.

RALPH: I see. Except I don't. Logically speaking just how is he going to do that more than half a century after he died?

VIVIAN: Don't you know? He was a really, really true believer in spirits and their ability to come back from the dead. When he sees two of his cousins in trouble, he'll help us. He wasn't the world's greatest escape artist for nothing.

RALPH: I'm sorry. I can't take any more of this. None of it makes sense to me. I'm Ralph Wise a not-so-nice Jewish boy from New York City, not Thomas Wyatt. Like you said when we first met, you're Vivian White from the same place as me. Except you're not. You're from some place I can never know. As much fun as this has been, I think it's time for me to leave now.

VIVIAN: Just like Wyatt did, but I shall truly miss you.

[ACOUSTIC: *Jet plane landing.*]

GARY: You didn't miss me, did you?

VIVIAN: I've found ways to keep busy.

GARY: You hardly noticed I was gone.

VIVIAN: Even when you're here, part of you stays at a distance.

GARY: If you really wanted to be close, you'd come with m on some of my trips.

You could come. Show everyone you believed in me.

VIVIAN: I'm always happy to come.

GARY: You're doing something behind my back, aren't you?

VIVIAN: Surely you're not implying that I've cast a spell, that I bewitched you.

GARY: Don't pull any more of your cute word games on me. I've had enough of them to last me two life times.

VIVIAN: I'm sorry you're not in the mood to play.

GARY: Play? God damn it, I've been the butt of your little games. For months. That's it. That's all I'm going to take from you.

VIVIAN: But you see, dear heart, you have nothing to give.

GARY: Give? You ungrateful little cur. At least the real Ann appreciated her boost in status when she married a king. Right to her end, she appreciated that.

VIVIAN: Somehow becoming Mrs. Professor Gary Pine didn't give me the same upward thrust Ann got.

GARY: Without me no one would've paid any attention to you. Do you think any publisher would have even looked at your crap if I hadn't put a word in for you? Go on, admit it. If it hadn't been for me, nobody but your three best friends, if you had them, would even know your name.

VIVIAN: Ann comes alive through me. You have precious little to do with it. Henry couldn't keep Ann in what he fancied was her place. He wasn't smart enough, so he cut off her head. Is that what you have in mind?

GARY: Well, let's just see. I'm getting the hell out of here. Want some witchcraft? I'll give you some witchcraft. I'll make you vanish. By the time I revisit the scene of your crime, for everyone who matters, you'll have disappeared from the sight. There'll be no head worth cutting off.

> [ACOUSTIC: *Gary stomps out. He slams the door behind him. A jet plane takes off.*]

END OF SCENE 16

Scene 17

Scene: *Ralph's living room.*

> [ACOUSTIC: *Knock at the door.*]

RALPH: Just a second!

> [ACOUSTIC: *Ralph walks to the door and opens it.*]

Where the hell have you been?

> [ACOUSTIC: *Gary walks in*]

GARY: I had to get out of there. I couldn't stand being in the same house with her any more.

RALPH: So move into a hotel. How could you just disappear for half a semester and not let anybody know?

GARY: I needed to go to London. I needed to get in better touch with my inner Henry. By the time I got back, she'd already changed the locks. She won't let me in. All my clothes and my laptop with my notes, all my notes. They're still in there.

RALPH: You might've let someone know where you were.

GARY: Henry didn't do telephones or email. It would have pulled me in the wrong direction.

RALPH: How about something old fashioned like leaving a note? I've been making excuses for you, but not very successfully.

GARY: And exactly how have I contributed to your lack of success?

RALPH: By graphically demonstrating to everyone something's up, or rather not up.

GARY: What do you mean?

RALPH: Come here. You'd better see this Instagram post. Near as I can tell, everyone else has.

> [ACOUSTIC: *Garry and Ralph walk to the desk. A desktop computer gets turned on.*]

GARY: Well screw her! Ralph, you've got to make her take that off the web. You tell her I'll sue.

RALPH: She used Henry VIII's head on what everyone presumes is your naked body and that means it gets classified as a work of art. You can sue, but you'll just draw more the attention to it. And you'll lose.

GARY: So you tell me how to handle this.

RALPH: Logically speaking, it seems to me there are two "thises" here. The short term one we just discussed. And there's nothing you can do. So let's apply some logic and be optimistic about a long term one where you've got some choices.

GARY: Long term?

RALPH: Yeah, are you gone from her life for just a few weeks or are you gone forever?

GARY: Do you mean divorce her? God, no. I can't face another divorce. I just can't.

RALPH: Any chance the two of you might patch it up?

GARY: About as much chance as Henry and Ann patching things up after he found out that she was screwing her brother.

RALPH: I'd forgotten about that. I guess there are worse fates than being Wyatt.

GARY: Yeah, Henry let the cousin live, but what are you talking about?

RALPH: Never mind. Well, if you can't be together and you can't be apart, it's hard to think of another choice.

GARY: She's not getting away with this. It's time my life and my scholarship began runnin' on the same track.

RALPH: How do you plan to do that?

GARY: It's my house, my palace, and they're my worldly goods. She's the one who needs to get out, and I'll take a great deal of pleasure in throwing her out.

RALPH: Things have been real quiet over at your place these past few days. Haven't even caught a glimpse of Vivian. In the interest of keeping things as they are currently, why don't you spend the night here? Then you could talk to a lawyer in the morning about getting Vivian to leave. It's your logical next move.

GARY: No, I'm the one who's in charge. I don't need any damn lawyers. Kill all the lawyers. I'll take care of it myself.

RALPH: Right now, in the middle of the night, that's not a real good idea. Just be logical, be sensible about this.

GARY: This is my life and your logic has nothing to do with it.

RALPH: If I were you, I really wouldn't go over there now.

GARY: Well, you're not me, are you? I'm Henry the God damn eighth and no one's going to tell me what to do.

> [ACOUSTIC: *Footsteps and then the door slams.*]

END OF SCENE 17

Scene 18

Scene: *Outside Gary and Vivian's house.*

> [ACOUSTIC: *"Greensleeves riff played under whole scene. Loud pounding on the door.*]

GARY: [*Yelling*] This is my house! You can't keep me out! I'm the king!

> [ACOUSTIC: *More banging.*]

You're the one who's gotta to get out! You hear me! I know you hear me!

> [ACOUSTIC: *Even louder banging.*]

You listen to me. I'm coming!

> [ACOUSTIC: *Another bang.*]

Whether you like it or not. Even if I have to crawl through that skylight on the roof. I'm coming!

> [ACOUSTIC: *Yet more pounding on the door.*]

Forgot about the skylight, didn't yah? Bet yah forgot the ladder too. I'm coming!

> [ACOUSTIC: *Ladder dragged to and slammed against the house. Sound of steps going up ladder and then across the roof. Gary slips and falls off the roof with a scream. Glass table shatters.*]

END OF SCENE 18

Scene 19

Scene: *Outside Gary's house.*

> [ACOUSTIC: *Ambulance siren starts loud and then fades. Ralph gasps several times.*]

POLICE: Don't rush. Take your time. Breathe deep.

RALPH: [*After taking a couple of deep breaths*] I can't stop shaking.

POLICE: Look, no civilian should have to see someone with what's left of his head sticking through a table. But the EMT told me he was a friend of yours and you found him. That right?

RALPH: [*Takes one more deep breathe.*] That's right, officer.

POLICE: So I gotta ask. Do you know what he was doin' on the roof in the middle of the night? Was this his house?

RALPH: In a way he was on the roof because it was his house.

POLICE: What do yah mean because it's his house?

RALPH: Doesn't make sense, does it?

POLICE: No, it don't, but that's the way it goes. Us cops run into people all the time who do stupid stuff.

RALPH: Reason is the slave of passion and can never pretend any other office.

POLICE: Come again?

RALPH: Some really, really smart guy wrote that when George Washington was around. Right now it seems to me he got it right.

POLICE: Oh.

END OF SCENE 19

Scene 20

Scene: *Eleanor's office.*

> [ACOUSTIC: *Al knocks on the door and without waiting for an answer, it opens and he walks in.*]

AL: You've heard, haven't you?

ELEANOR: And hello to you too, Al.

AL: Sorry, but haven't you?

ELEANOR: Is there anybody on campus who hasn't? Gary, that poor, hopeless man. I wouldn't wish what happened to him on anyone.

AL: And Ralph, finding him lying there. It must've been awful. And Vivian, what happened to Vivian? I heard she wasn't even home, hasn't been around for a while. Does anyone know where she is?

ELEANOR: Vivian? Oh she's gone. Left a few days before Gary came back from London.

AL: What?

ELEANOR: She locked up the house and took off.

AL: You're pullin' my leg.

ELEANOR: No. Really, really. Apparently she's been planning this for some time. She asked me to keep it quiet 'till she got settled in.

AL: Settled in where?

ELEANOR: Hollywood. She's left the university for more creative undertakings. She's been planning it for some time.

AL: Do you mind telling me, what in the world she'll do. In Hollywood. Creative undertakings? All she has is a PhD in lit. She could starve.

ELEANOR: She has a job.

AL: As a waitress?

ELEANOR: As a paid consultant for a production company that's doing *Ann of a Thousand Days* on one of those streaming channels. And a bio-pic on Harry Houdini. No one knows them better.

AL: But what about Ralph? I've been too chicken to ask him anything.

ELEANOR: He's been in his office, pretending to do some work.

AL: He's gotta feel like hell.

ELEANOR: Turns out the world wasn't as logical as he wanted it to be. Nothing like having everything you believed turn out to be a pipedream. But, shall I tell you what I have in mind for him?

AL: Please.

ELEANOR: A comedy.

AL: There is a good one showing in town?

ELEANOR: There will be. And with a bit of luck, he'll be in it.

AL: What are you talking about?

ELEANOR: That play I'm directing, *Much Ado About Nothing*. It's taken me forever, but I've got the whole thing cast except for lead guy, Benedick. The part's made for Ralph.

AL: I don't know. Acting in a play ? Isn't that way out of his comfort zone?

ELEANOR: That's the idea. Shakespeare to the rescue. His characters are so deliciously human. That should get our friend out of that slough of despond he's been occupying.

AL: How's being in a play going to give him a way to get things turned right side up when his world's upside down?

ELEANOR: By throwing himself into becoming Benedick. If there ever was a character who he had his world and the woman in it turned upside down, it's him. Yet by the end of the play Benedick turns into a happy new man.

AL: Eleanor, Eleanor do you really think you can turn Ralph, the caterpillar, into Ralph, the butterfly?

ELEANOR: Maybe not, but I'm sure going to try.

[ACOUSTIC: *"Scarborough Fair"*]

END OF SCENE 20

Scene 21

Scene: *Civic Theater stage.*

ELEANOR: Ralph, don't worry about where to stand on the stage. For now, just say your lines.

RALPH: "One woman is fair, yet I am well; another is wise, yet I am well; another is virtuous, yet I am well."

ELEANOR: Try it again. Don't over-think it. How does Benedick feel about women?

RALPH: "One woman is fair, yet I am well; another is wise, yet I am well; another virtuous, yet I am well."

ELEANOR: Not there yet. Feel the words. Make them yours.

RALPH: Make myself into Benedick?

ELEANOR: That's right. See the world through Benedick's eyes,

RALPH: "One woman is fair, yet I am well; another is wise, yet I am well; another virtuous, yet I am well; but till all graces be in one woman, one woman shall not come in my grace.

ELEANOR: Why Ralph, you've made me believe in butterflies.

[ACOUSTIC: *"Scarborough Fair"*]

END OF PLAY